I0006851

Strategic Excellence in Post-Digital Ecosystems: A B2C Perspective

Edin Güçlü Sözer

Mustafa Emre Civelek

Murat Çemberci

Zea Books
2018

Copyright © 2018 Edin Güçlü Sözer,
Mustafa Emre Civelek, and Murat Çemberci.

Composed in Sitka types.

ISBN 978-1-60962-125-4

doi 10.13014/K2TT4P4C
https://doi.org/10.13014/K2TT4P4C

Zea Books are published by
the University of Nebraska–Lincoln Libraries

Electronic (pdf) edition online at
http://digitalcommons.unl.edu/zeabook/

Print edition sold at
http://www.lulu.com/spotlight/unlib

UNL does not discriminate based upon any protected status.
Please go to unl.edu/nondiscrimination

Preface

Each and every day, enterprises are making business processes more efficient; this is possible because of revolutionary developments in information technologies. At the same time, however, these developments seriously threaten the economic order, reducing the demand for labor as existing jobs are taken over by machines. Developments in information technologies have also introduced more uncertainty in the economic environment. This new economic model is known as the digital economy. "Digitalization" refers to its use of information technology in all business processes. "Digital divides" occur between individuals who use information technologies and those who cannot. A digital divide may occur between countries or between individuals. The criteria for judging the digitalization of countries are internet penetration and speed of internet access; the criteria for assessing the digitalization of individuals are telephone subscription, computer ownership, access to broadband internet, and internet usage time. The basic production of this digital economy is knowledge. The relative weight of the production factors of classical economic theory has changed. The importance of knowledge and entrepreneurship has increased, while the importance of labor and capital is decreasing. Unemployment is rising in an unstoppable way, from the persistent loss of employment for production, and the conversion of labor to consumption is becoming increasingly difficult.

Individuals who use technology effectively in the digital economy have relatively higher incomes than those in more labor-intensive sectors. The digital divide becomes an increasingly important issue as the share of electronic commerce increases in proportion to the total volume of trade. E-commerce is, in fact, the most important driving force of the digital economy,

This book deals with the new concepts determining the future path of e-commerce and aims at providing a new perspective to the field.

Contents

About the Authors

Edin Güçlü SÖZER is an assistant professor in the Faculty of Business and Administrative Sciences at Okan University. In addition to his academic background, he has also managed retail marketing, sales, and business development functions for local and multinational banks for more than two decades and has participated in many leading international projects. He earned his Ph.D. degree in marketing in 2008. His publications include books (Internet Commerce-2003, Post-Modern Marketing-2009, and Dynamics of Sponsorship-2010) as well as articles and research papers in academic journals. In addition to his previous mandates in finance sector, he also serves on the Editorial Board of *Journal of International Trade, Logistics and Law* (JITAL) and Board of Reviewers of *International Journal of Commerce and Finance* (IJCF).

Mustafa Emre CİVELEK is an assistant professor in the Faculty of Business Administration at Istanbul Commerce University and the Board Member of Technologistics Application & Research Center. Between the years 2012-2017, he was the head of the Ground Handling Services Management in Aviation Program. He teaches courses in e-commerce, foreign trade, and logistics. He has Ph.D. degree in business administration. He earned his undergraduate degree from Istanbul Technical University in 1994 and a master's degree from Yeditepe University in 2002. He is also a Practitioner, working from 1994 until 2008 in the banking industry, mainly in international trade finance operations. His focus, therefore, concerns bridging the gap between theory and practice. His academic publications include books and academic papers on several issues regarding e-commerce and management.

Murat ÇEMBERCİ is an assistant professor in the Faculty of Business Administration at Istanbul Commerce University, where he teaches courses in Management and Organization, Business Administration, Entrepreneurship, and Logistics. He earned his undergraduate degree from Uludağ University in 2006 and masters and Ph.D. degrees from Gebze Technical University in 2011. During those same years, he also worked as a manager in the logistics sector. At Istanbul Commerce University since 2012, his research and publications focus on R&D and innovation, innovation management, entrepreneurship, purchasing and supply chain management, and international transportation.

1. Introduction

Digitalization was introduced to the business world in the 1960s and has accelerated since the emergence of e-commerce in the 1990s. E-commerce has become the main driver of the digital economy and has gained a much greater share of the world's trade volume. The developments in the retail business are particularly noteworthy. The share of the e-commerce within the total trade is increasing quite fast. Development of e-commerce within the global trade has triggered radical changes in the business processes. Electronic business applications are now being used in all functions of the business. This situation requires competition to be reshaped. While competition took place between business managements in the past, it has recently developed among the supply chains, and information management has emerged as the new field of competition today. As the most important production factor of the digital economy, information is now the key instrument that enables enterprises to jump ahead of the competition.

Today, drastic gaps of information access are emerging between the users and non-users of the Internet. This poses a serious threat to societies that have not achieved digital development because of the risk that the gap with the developed countries will become unbridgeable. The Internet, emerging as a new technology, eradicates many business lines but does not create new jobs at the same rate, as it needs less labor than before. The effects of digitalization, however, will be felt in different dimensions between developed, developing, and underdeveloped countries because the effects of digitalization have sociological, cultural and social dimensions in addition to their economic dimension. For example, in developed countries that manage information, produce technology, and become highly digitalized, fewer human resources are needed due to increased productivity. Yet the new job areas that are created could recruit and balance the residual human resources. In a similar logic, in countries that cannot manage information, cannot produce technology, and have low levels of digitalization, human resource demands for operational purposes will continue for a while. When the global dimension is concerned, it can be said that the need for human resources (labor) will decrease if the digitalization increases with this pace.

This book, firstly, makes a review of the evolution of digitalization from the emergence of information technologies and to Industry 4.0 and then provides information on the electronic work models. It touches upon the management of the increasingly important e-commerce websites and then explains the post-digital ecosystem, as well as the strategies to be applied in this new system.

The aim of this book is to reveal the changes taking place in the organizational environment of commercial enterprises, changes that define the strategies they can implement. This book also offers some new definitions and introduces new concepts to the literature on e-commerce. The last part of the book explains what the enterprises should do to exist in this new economic system and digital world and provides useful information to share with business managers.

2. Evolution of Digitalization

Among the main dynamics having an impact on the emergence of e-commerce, the advances in the information technology come first. Originating in a military project in the 1960s, information technology has become a part of commercial life since the mid-1990s. This section covers the topics of the development of information technologies and internet, emergence of a new ecosocial system and the concept of industry 4.0.

2.1. Development of Information Technology

Information technology has begun to be used for the very first time by the widespread use of the internet by companies. The Internet has increased the efficiency of information technologies used by these companies.

In today's fiercely competitive environment, the ability of companies to gain a competitive advantage can be said to be largely related to their ability to collect data, convert the collected data into information, and use this information efficiently. Since the effectiveness of decision-making increases in those enterprises that produce information and use it effectively for problem-solving, their organizational goals can be achieved more rapidly. According to Bresnahan, information technology in today's businesses has gone beyond a support function and has begun instead to play a strategic role. These technology developments have contributed to the management, production factors, and the efficiency of enterprises and have become an indispensable element for them. Today, information technology is seen as a strategic resource (Bresnahan, 2002).

At the beginning of the nineties, some opposing views were also put forward. For example, in his study of 1993, Brynjolfsson introduced a concept called technology efficiency. In the study, he argued that information technology did not always deliver the expected productivity gains to the business, on the contrary, it caused the productivity to decrease. It is concluded in the research that use of information technologies did not necessarily yield benefit to the enterprises (Brynjolfsson E., 1993). To Daft, the information systems can be separated into two basic groups as follows:

The first one is the operational information systems: Systems in which the daily transactions are carried out and recorded in operational levels in the enterprises. Office automation systems, transaction recording systems and process control systems can be noted as examples (Daft, 1997).

The second one is the management information systems: Systems which are used by the managers in fulfilling the managerial functions. They can be exemplified as the high-level information support systems, information systems, and information reporting systems. The use of information technologies makes a positive contribution to the organization to get harmonized with the environment and to make prompt response to the changes around.

The studies made since the 1960s have shown that technological developments have increased the share of the managerial workforce within the organization because those technological developments caused non-qualified workforce in routine jobs to lose their jobs rapidly. (Lee, 1964)

In today's organizations, the horizontal communication is made via information systems, and the use of information systems increases the information exchange. The information systems remove the locational restrictions and enable the employees from different departments, and even geographies, to work together by forming virtual teams. The virtual teams are those which are independent of time, space and company borders (Berry, 2011).

These information technologies continue to evolve. While they were used initially as operational information systems, in time they began to be used as managerial information systems as well. Today, the information systems have turned out to be strategic assets. These strategic systems can be diverted into two categories: internal coordination and external coordination. Examples of those used for internal coordination are intranets, corporation resource planning and information management systems. Examples of those used for external communication are extranets, integrated business systems, and supply chain management systems (Daft, Organization Theory and Design, 2004).

The "supply chain management systems" — defined as the integrated systems which make integration of all external elements like customers, suppliers, dealers, transporters with the organization — are important for the effectiveness of companies today. These electronic business systems are described as strategic arms with a dramatic articulation (Siau & Tian, 2004).

2.2. Development of Internet

The internet, indeed, is a military product which emerged in the cold war between the United States of America (US) and the Union of Soviet Socialist Republics (USSR). The deepening disagreements between the US and the USSR in the aftermath of the Second World War led to the cold war the 1947-1962 period. The political and economic rivalry among the two forces peaked in this period. Since the consequences of a nuclear war would have been catastrophic for both sides, the war was waged in the field of propaganda. Scientific advances were used a propaganda instrument in this period. The US decided to move forward after the success of the USSR's Sputnik project delivered the first satellite to space. The Advanced Research Projects Agency (ARPA) was established in 1958 by the US Department of Defense. When the USSR deployed nuclear-head missiles to Cuba, ARPA was assigned to set up a new communication network.

The main goal was to enable US bases around the world to keep their communication in the event of a nuclear war. The planned computer network should be center-free and open to the connection in different ways. If a computer center is a target, other centers should keep communication. This is the reason the internet's center-free structure cannot be terminated by states even today (Barron, Ellsworth, & Savetz, 1997).

In 1958, the ARPA was assigned the mission to develop a method connect two computers in different regions. The packet-switching method was developed by ARPA after scientific research. This method makes the data to be broken into pieces before sending and to be reunified at the point of arrival. Every package can reach to the address individually or even with different ways, and at the point of arrival it is re-compiled, and the original message is thereby created. The TCP/IP, today's the basic internet protocol, uses the packet-switching. In 1963, the US air forces started research on a center-free network which could maintain control of military forces in the event of nuclear attack. ARPA supported the project, and the project was called as ARPANET. The first technological development of internet was started with the ARPANET project and the research on the packet-switching (Barron, Ellsworth, & Savetz, 1997). The developed technology was presented to the disposal of the civilians after the nuclear threat disappeared. The first physical network was established in California. The work was carried out by an institution called BBN and four points among Stanford Research Institute, UCLA, Utah, and UC Santa Barbara were connected to each other. Figure 1 shows the 1969 version of the ARPANET.

The number of computers connected to the Internet reached 23 in 1971, and the use of the internet as an electronic post office commenced. This feature has played a key role in the huge global expansion of the internet today. An essential feature of the internet is that in case there is a breaking in the lines, the data can be transmitted via alternative resources (Barron, Ellsworth, & Savetz, 1997).

In 1972, the University of Utah developed the TELNET and became the first institution to control a remote computer via the internet. During this period, the FTP transfer protocol was developed. In 1979, the Computer Sciences Research Network was set up; it resembled ARPANET but was used only for the computer sciences.

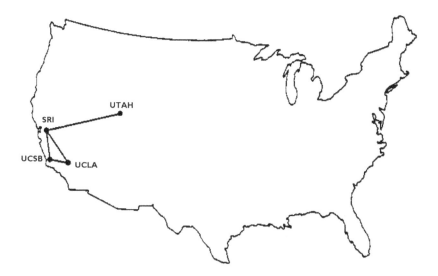

Figure 1. ARPANET 1969. Source: (Davesite, 2015)

In 1980, this network was connected to ARPANET (Barron, Ellsworth, & Savetz, 1997).

It was in 1982 that the phrase "internet" was first used. A wide network, called BITNET, was established at City University of New York in 1983. The first domain name server was developed at University of Wisconsin in the same year; this made it possible to give an easy-to-remember name, corresponding to the IP number, to the computers in the network. The seven high-level domain names were established as .gov, .edu, .mil, .int, .com, .org, .net. The number of computers connected to the internet reached 28,000 in 1987.

The most important development happened in 1991: Tim Berners-Lee, a CERN researcher, developed the HTTP protocol. This ushered in the era in which the web interface that we use today and the websites coded as HTML were developed. The number of computers connected to the internet reached 2 million in 1993, and there were 600 www websites. Commercial usage of the internet started in 1995. The number of hosts today has reached to 850 million, as seen in Figure 2 (Laudon & Traver, 2012).

The concepts of web and internet are different. The internet was developed in the early 1960s and is a network that connects computers. The web, developed in the early 1990s, is an interface for viewing the HTML documents. The web also has its distinct eras. The period between 1990 and 2000 is called the Web 1.0; it was a period of static web pages whose interaction with the user was quite limited.

The period between 2000 and 2010 is known as Web 2.0 (Serge, 2015). This is the period when sites were developed such as Wikipedia and Twitter, which interact with users and enable them to create content. The most important feature of the Web 2.0 is its dynamic structure. The dynamic feature means having interaction with the user. The popularity of web 2.0 sites by the early 2000s made consumers more knowledgeable, more conscious and demanding. The impact of consumer comments and complaints on the social networks regarding business's products and services poses threats for the enterprises, but it also provides an opportunity to get ahead of their rivals.

Web 3.0 is mainly concerned with robotics and artificial intelligence, and the adaptation of these works to the web domain means that the content on the internet can be understood by computers. It is also called the semantic web. The period we live in is called Web 3.0 (Civelek, 2009). The Internet has six basic features, summarized below (Civelek, 2009):

1. Center-free: The internet does not have a central computer. The information is transferred in packets with various ways. We can't stop the internet by shutting down some computers. This stems from internet's initial design as a military project.

2. Free: Although there are efforts to apply various bans, the users can overcome them in some way. The best example for this is that many illegal activities are increasingly conducted over the internet.

3. Global: The internet is not limited to a certain geography. The internet broadcast can be made to all world at the same time.

4. Dynamic: The visitors can also make a contribution and provide content. Sites using this feature are said to be Web 2.0 sites.

5. Borderless: It can't be stopped by the country borders. It prevents the political border. This feature negates any country's bans on sites.

6. Asynchronous: There is no requirement for synchronous watching or listening as it is on TV and radio broadcast. The broadcast can be watched from anywhere in the world without time limit.

2.3. Emergence of New Ecosocial System

The period we live in is named the "information age," and its societies are known the information society. As a result of the transformation of knowledge into a production factor, a phenomenon called the new ecosocial system has emerged. The new ecosocial system has strengthened the individual and removed obstacles in front of the entrepreneurship (Civelek, 2009). The characteristics of the information society underlying the new ecosocial system can be listed as follows (Genç, 2007):

1. Computers form the basis of the information society.

2. The leading sector is the information sector.

3. The importance and power of the concept of civil society have increased.

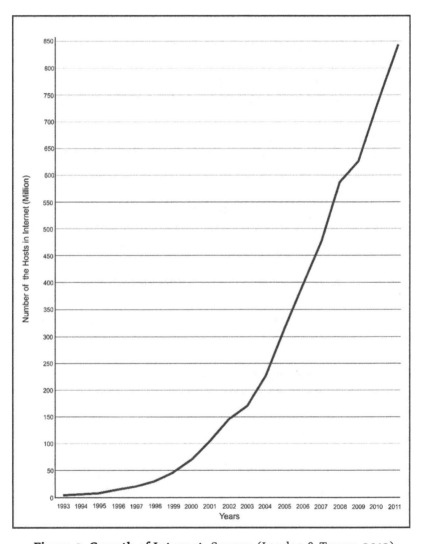

Figure 2. Growth of Internet. Source: (Laudon & Traver, 2012)

4. It is multi-centered.

5. The political system is a participatory democracy.

6. Unlike the industrial society producing consumer goods, it produces a lot of information.

7. The basic value in industrial society is the satisfaction of material needs. In the information society, fundamental value is achieving goals.

The new ecosocial system can be defined as the ever-changing economic and social system that includes new trade, business, communication and lifestyles that have come to the fore as a result of increased uncertainty in the technological environment and increasing global communication among the people through electronic networks (Civelek & Sözer, İnternet Ticareti: Yeni EkoSosyal Sistem ve Ticaret Noktaları, 2003).

It would be useful to address, one by one, the dynamic structure and the feature of the new ecosystem as well as its differences from the former economic system.

First of all, the new ecosocial system, in contrast to other economic systems regarding scope, carries both economic and social characteristics, or individual oriented characteristics in other words. Thanks to this feature, the system has created its social dynamism and is constantly in the process of renewal, by integrating its effects with its reaction. Thanks to multi-channel communication subsystems in the new ecosocial system, both individuals and institutions are connected to each other via electronic networks in national and international contexts, and this neural system has transformed the problem of communication into an opportunity. One of the most fundamental characteristics of the new ecosocial system is that it can save both individuals and corporations from being trapped in the national arena and provide an international maneuver space. Due to the borderless nature of the Internet, in the new ecosocial system the borders of the country have lost their significance. Today, individuals are expanding their social lives by communicating with each other in seconds all over the world and expanding the boundaries of national communication. When corporations are concerned, together with the new ecosocial system, the concept of the national market in the old economic order has given way to the concept of "Global Market," and this system has enabled corporations to trade globally. Another feature where the new ecosocial system differs from the old system is the renewal and automation of the laggard and ineffective work methods with the technological revolution. Today, both individuals and corporations use technological tools and models provided by the new ecosocial system in their way of doing business, and they are getting much more effective results. In the new ecosocial system, corporations act on the principle of "minimum cost maximum benefit" due to effective business models and technological speed, and thanks to the falling costs, they use these resources in different fields and become more efficient (Civelek, 2009).

The losses incurred by those who do not change their classical business methods and are not open to innovations leads to the elimination of enterprises that cannot adapt to the new ecosocial system. Although the decrease in the importance of labor in the new economic model triggers global unemployment and heralds a dark future, the effective use of information management systems in all sectors will increase global efficiency, decrease costs, and create more general welfare.

There are serious problems in some labor-intensive industries, such as agriculture. This has a negative impact particularly on the economies of countries reliant on those industries. However, if technological developments are incorporated into production processes in labor-intensive industries, there will be no loss of production, thanks to improved efficiency. Nevertheless, there will be human-origin problems, although these may be solved by developments in the new economic system. Thousands of new business lines are created each year in developed countries that have an impact in the world economy. With this in mind, human resources are employed most accurately in countries targeting efficiency and effectiveness in the production processes. Therefore, generating, acquiring, and managing knowledge are crucial for companies to achieve sustainable performance in a competitive environment (Civelek, Çemberci, Kibritci Artar, & Uca, 2015).

The dynamics of the new ecosocial system diverges from the old system regarding the impact of change and ambiguity on enterprises. This change can best be observed in the creative destruction impact of the internet. Creative destruction is a phenomenon precipitated by the internet in almost all businesses today. The concept of creative destruction was developed in the early 20th century by Joseph Schumpeter (1883–1950), an Austrian thinker. Creative destruction can be defined as the destruction of existing business lines by new technology or innovation and the replacement of them with new business fields (Wadhwani, 2012). The new ecosocial system realizes creative destruction in a way different from what Schumpeter defines. The internet, as a new technology, eliminates many business lines but does not create the same number of jobs, since its new businesses require less labor. This puts workers in industries like music and media under serious threat today.

One of the most important issues to be highlighted is that companies who have achieved gains in this new ecosocial system change process are not guaranteed to succeed in the market. Because of rapid changes in the system, companies that seems to be very successful today and have a high share of the market are still at risk of losing their leadership position to their rivals or of being completely dragged out of the competition due to sudden responses of consumers and competitors.

On the other hand, a company located in the bottom rung of the market can make the right moves and jump in front of its competitors. These features of the system force companies to take risks, and this new ecosystem requires them to continue to take and bear risks for continuous success (Civelek, Çemberci, Kibritci Artar, & Uca, 2015).

Today, Amazon's success is the result of assuming the market risks of this new ecosocial system. If these risks had not been not taken, and the opening up first to all of America and then to the whole world had not been realized, "Amazon" would still be a local company selling online books in Seattle today. Within the new ecosocial system, risk and success are tied closer than ever before. In other words, the success and market leadership of the companies in the new ecosocial system today is based on a logical risk-taking strategy, while the success of companies in the old economy system was based on assuming less risk (Civelek & Sözer, 2003).

Environmental uncertainty is not a new concept, despite the fact that it has grown after the introduction of the internet into business life. Particularly towards the end of the eighties, uncertainty has grown with the influence of globalization and the developments in information systems. Environmental uncertainty is an external force on the performance of the operator. Even before the impact of the Internet, the market had begun to become more global and customer-focused, and the demands of customers had become more variable, quality-focused and fast-delivery oriented (Thomas & Griffin, 1996). Today, the product life cycle is getting shorter and technological developments are getting faster. Enterprises need to establish strategic partnerships, especially with the suppliers, to adapt to this uncertain environment (Krause, Handfield, & Scannel, 1998).

In the period just before the introduction of internet, environmental uncertainties had already emerged with the rise of externalities such as the increase in global competition and the development of new technologies. These factors made existing products out of date more rapidly and changed customer demands and requirements, which shortened the product life cycle (Gupta & Wilemon, 1990). The internet increases these effects exponentially.

Environmental uncertainty is caused by unexpected changes in customers and technology. Customer uncertainty can be defined as unpredictable changes in customers' demands and preferences. Especially with the emergence of social media, the consumer has become more active than ever. The same customer who can reach the product information very quickly can also share his complaints very effectively on the internet. Customer demands for products and services have become increasingly vague regarding time, volume and location. Today, customers demand more options, better service, higher quality and faster delivery (Civelek, Çemberci, Kibritci Artar, & Uca, 2015).

Technology uncertainty can be defined as unpredictable changes in technology. Developments in information technology include opportunities as well as threats for commercial enterprises. Recent advances in internet technologies have opened up opportunities for companies to increase their effectiveness, especially in supply chain integration. What is important here is to move faster and earlier than the competitors (Poirier & Bauer, 2001). These advanced information systems reduce transaction costs associated with product flow control and provide faster response to customer needs (Li & Lin, 2006).

The most important production factor in the new ecosocial system — what will provide a competitive advantage to enterprises in the environment of today's uncertainty — is knowledge. The enterprise's focus on knowledge management is the most important factor in providing a competitive advantage. For enterprises, formatting the information in a way to create commercial value and applying it in line with organizational goals are as important as generating the information itself. In this context, generating information will not be enough, but giving initiative and freedom to individuals in the application of this information will play a key role in the success. In many business ideas, there are significant differences between the original conception and the resulting product. For this reason, it is necessary for the teams making an innovation to be responsible for the commercialization of the implementation of the idea, and to move freely, on the condition of not being outside the enterprise's goals. (Çemberci, 2012).

In generating new ideas within the enterprise, inter-team cooperation and cooperation with enterprise shareholders are very important, as well as the cooperation of team members. The inclusion of new customers and suppliers to the new idea generation process is extremely important for the success and dissemination of the idea.

Since creation of innovations within the company will create the value most suitable for the company structure, it will give much more successful results than innovations adopted from outside. For this reason, the creation of an organization culture that supports innovation and change within the company will yield much more productive results in the long run.

"Choosing" is to decide which of the ideas developed within an organization will be implemented. This decision-making process is extremely critical and can be said to be the most important phase of the innovation process. This decision-making process — which innovative idea is chosen among the interest areas of various political structures — is not as easy as it might seem. It will not be surprising if radical, innovative ideas that might be very useful for the enterprise are rejected because of political reasons. Effective ideas can only be adopted through the unconditional support of top management. For this reason, the successful selection process is directly executed by the senior management itself (Lu & Yang, 2004).

In the stage of idea development, the mission should be given to the person or groups who have raised the idea. At this stage, senior management support and the necessary resources should be given to the team that will develop the idea. Since the original idea may go in very different directions at the idea development stage, teams should have the necessary freedom and the support of senior management at all stages, as innovation will touch various political divisions within the enterprise.

The dissemination phase is the implementation of the developed idea within the company. Because of potential serious resistance at this stage, there is a need for decisive support from top management, as there was in the previous stages. Otherwise, business ideas that are revealed and developed after intensive labor may disappear without debut. In the new ecosocial system, the best response from management to environmental uncertainty is to create an environment that supports information production within the enterprise (Civelek and Çemberci, 2015).

2.4. Industry 4.0

Technological advances have pioneered industry from the beginning (TÜSİAD, 2016). The term Industry 4.0 refers to a further developmental stage in the organization and management of the entire value chain process involved in the manufacturing industry. Another term of this precess is the fourth industrial revolution (Delloite, Challenges, and Solutions for the digital transformation and use of exponential Technologies, 2015). Industrial production was transformed by steam power in the nineteenth-century, by electricity in the early twentieth century, and by automation in the 1970s. These waves of technological advancements, however, did not reduce overall employment. Although the number of manufacturing jobs decreased, new jobs emerged, and the demand for new skills grew. Today another workforce transformation is on the horizon as manufacturing experiences a fourth way of technological advancements: the rise of new digital industrial technologies that are collectively known as Industry 4.0 (BCG, 2015).

2.4.1. Development of the Concept

Bledowski has suggested that the origins of the idea are to be found in the German government's 2006 High-Tech Strategy. Some of the features of Industry 4.0 were identified in Germany's industrial policy in 2010, and in 2012 the government made Industry 4.0 one of 10 future projects in its High-Tech Strategy. A working group consisting of representatives from industry, academics, and science was set up by the German Ministry of Education and Research. In 2013 they published a final report outlining eight priorities of an Industry 4.0 strategy, ranging from standardization to continued learning.

The Ministry of Economics stated the goal of fostering research and innovation "at a precompetitive stage" and accelerating the process of transferring scientific findings into the development of marketable technologies. That this not only concerns large corporations becomes clear when the strategy explicitly includes the goal of strengthening the innovation power of entrepreneurs and small and medium-sized enterprises (SMEs) by creating competence centers for Industry 4.0.

The German government has since institutionalized its commitment to Industry 4.0 by setting up a platform led by Ministries of Economy and Research bringing together representatives from business, science, and the trade unions. The Industry 4.0 platform has divided up its main areas of focus across five different working groups: Reference Architecture; Standardization; Research and Innovation; Networked Systems Security; Legal Environment; and Work, Education/Training. The platform issued the first report in April 2015. This report introduced the utility of Industry 4.0 to the wider economy and society as one of the key aspects to be further explored in the future and outlined a more refined research roadmap until 2030. This time horizon shows that Industry 4.0 is a very long-term strategy and that the transformation it seeks to foster is still in embryonic form (European Parliament, 2016). Industry 4.0 has emerged when machines start to manage themselves and production processes without the need for human power. Industry 4.0 was first mentioned at the Hannover Messe trade fair in 2011.

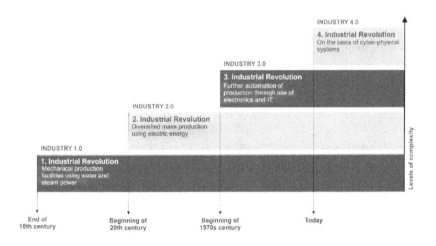

Figure 3. Industrial Revolutions

Source: (Social Innovation Policy for Industry 4.0, 2017)

As your organization moves toward Industry 4.0 readiness, you'll face countless decisions about the integration of new technologies, along with updates to current systems and processes. These decisions can be expensive, such as when your enterprise selects new manufacturing logistics software. To ensure that your decisions will position you well to evolve toward Industry 4.0, focus on four key concepts:

- **Information transparency:** Industry 4.0 systems create a "cyber-physical system," where the physical world is quantified into contextual, accessible data. Systems seamlessly and instantly share that data as required, ensuring that all systems cooperate using real-time information. Any new technology your company adopts should offer this transparency.

- **Interoperability:** In an Industry 4.0 system, it's possible for people, machines, sensors and devices to connect and communicate with one another. This facet of Industry 4.0 requires supply chain managers to take a broader perspective on compatibility requirements for software, machines and other devices.

- **Decentralized decision making:** Currently most supply chains operate using centralized decision making. But Industry 4.0 has brought a new level of autonomy, where systems will be able to make simple decisions on their own. This has the potential to increase efficiency by reducing time and resources allocated for centralized oversight.

- **Technical assistance:** Automation and robots already provide vital support in environments that are too treacherous for humans. The next phase is building a system that can support humans in decision-making and problem-solving. This interdependence of systems and humans is a key feature of Industry 4.0

While the sweeping impact of Industry 4.0 may not be obvious for five to ten years, the impact on supply chain management is already visible today. As supply chain managers look to the future, they should look to Industry 4.0 as a foundation (Flexis, 2017).

2.4.2. What is Industry 4.0?

The term "Industrie 4.0" was initially coined by the German government. It describes and encapsulates a set of technological changes in manufacturing and sets out priorities of a coherent policy framework with the aim of maintaining the global competitiveness of German industry. It is conceptual in that it sets out a way of understanding an observed phenomenon and institutional in that it provides the framework for a range of policy initiatives identified and supported by government and business representatives that drive a research and development program.

Industry 4.0 describes the organization of production processes based on technology and devices autonomously communicating with each other along the value chain: a model of the 'smart' factory of the future where computer-driven systems monitor physical processes, create a virtual copy of the physical world and make decentralized decisions based on self-organization mechanisms. The concept takes account of the increased computerization of the manufacturing industries where physical objects are seamlessly integrated into the information network. As a result, "manufacturing systems are vertically networked with business processes within factories and enterprises and horizontally connected to spatially dispersed value networks that can be managed in real time – from the moment an order is placed right through to outbound logistics." These developments make the distinction between industry and services less relevant as digital technologies are connected with industrial products and services into hybrid products which are neither goods nor services exclusively. Indeed, both the terms 'Internet of Things' and 'Internet of Services' are considered elements of Industry 4.0 (European Parliament, 2016).

Industry 4.0 is currently more vision than reality, but it is already poised to change not only the way we do business but our social cohesion in general. Industry 4.0 is the vision of increasing digitization of production. The concept describes how the so-called Internet of things, data and services will change in future production, logistics and work processes (Acatech, 2014). In this context, industry representatives also like to talk about a fourth industrial revolution. They are alluding to a new organization and steering of the entire value chain, which is increasingly becoming aligned with individual customer demands. The value chain thus has to cover the entire lifecycle of a product, from the initial idea through the task of developing and manufacturing it to successive customer delivery as well as the product's recycling, all the while integrating the associated services (Social Innovation Policy for Industry 4.0, 2017).

According to another definition, Industry 4.0 is a high-tech strategy that promotes the computerization of the manufacturing industry. The goal is the intelligent or smart factory, which is characterized by adaptability, resource efficiency, and ergonomics as well as the integration of customers and business partners in business and value processes.

The technological strategy is based on cyber-physical systems and the Internet of Things. Industry 4.0 has its roots in Germany but is spreading worldwide to other industrialized nations, including the U.S (Intel, 2015).

In the future, objects could communicate with each other directly and independently (see figure 3). They consult one another about what should happen to them next. This means that objects will become machine-readable. Even those that have yet to be outfitted with electronic components will receive their IP addresses. Internet protocol IPv6 makes this possible, as it offers a much greater number of potential addresses and easier encryption as well as authenticity verification (Social Innovation Policy for Industry 4.0, 2017).

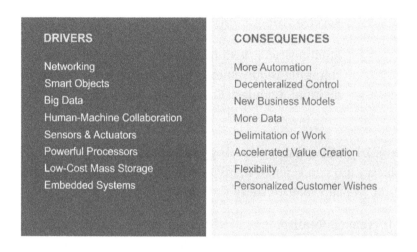

Figure 4. Drivers and Consequences of Industry 4.0
Source: (Social Innovation Policy for Industry 4.0, 2017)

The main features of Industry 4.0 are:

- Interoperability: cyber-physical systems (workpiece carriers, assembly stations and products) allow humans and smart factories to connect and communicate with each other.

- Virtualization: a virtual copy of the Smart Factory is created by linking sensor data with virtual plant models and simulation models.

- Decentralization: the ability of cyber-physical systems to make decisions of their own and to produce locally thanks to technologies such as 3-D printing.

- Real-Time Capability: the capability to collect and analyze data and provide the derived insights immediately,

- Service Orientation.

- Modularity: a flexible adaptation of smart factories to changing requirements by replacing or expanding individual modules (European Parliament, 2016).

2.4.3. Digitalization Technology in Industry 4.0

Industry 4.0 can refer to many technologies that enable digitalization. We can refer to these as follows.

Increased Reality: It is a vivid image created by enriching data such as sound, image, graphic, GPS generated by the computer in the real world. The reality is changed by the computer and enhanced. The user may interact with information around it.

Layered Manufacturing/3D Printers: It is the use of 3D printing methods to transform computer aided engineering designs into fully functional and durable objects made up of different materials.

Internet of Things (IoT): Objects that have a digital network and the internet must acquire a virtual identity and communicate in a physical and social sense with the environment.

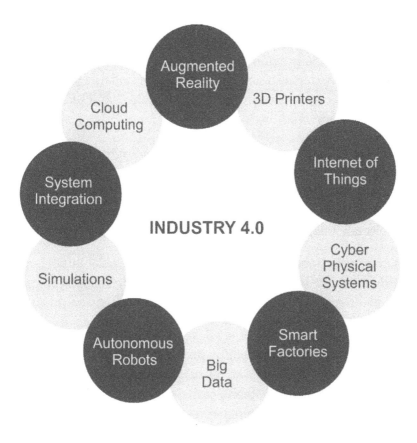

Figure 5.Digitalization Technology in Industry 4.0
Source: (Global Industry 4.0 Survey, 2016)

Cyber-Physical Systems: Cyber-Physical Systems are systems in which the basic principles of production processes such as observation, coordination, and control are governed by hybrid technology, which consists of a combination of computation and communication. It is to make the physical machines smarter by integration with cyber technology.

Smart Factories: For customizable products, intelligent electronic systems with internet connection are used in the production process to provide production-related advantages; Flexible and dynamic, self-coordinating and optimizing production by creating a large communication network among the production elements.

Big Data: It is a concept used to define the volume, variety, speed and value of information. It includes technologies for transforming all collected data from sources such as social media shares, blogs, and photos, and videos into meaningful and workable information.

Otonom Robots/Artificial Intelligence: Artificial intelligence provides solutions to complex problems by mimicking human thought and reaching autonomous motion systems in this way.

Simulation: It is a model in which appropriate outputs can be obtained when the system or processes containing the relations defined between systems components are fed with specified inputs. After the steam, electricity, and information powers that have entered the business world during the previous three industrial revolutions, simulation technology now also enters the factory.

System Integration: More than one system can be brought together to work as a single system. While products are being designed, they need to be developed in such a way that different systems and components can integrate with each other and with other systems.

Cloud Computing: All the applications, programs and data are stored in a virtual server, that is to say in the cloud, and when they are connected to the internet, the services through which they can be easily accessed through the devices are called Cloud Computing.

2.4.4. Industry 4.0 and its Consequences for the World of Work
According to a survey by Staufen AG in 2015, the development status of the countries in the world in Industry 4.0 is shown in the following graphic (Global Industry 4.0 Survey, 2016).

According to a survey conducted by PwC with the participation of 2,000 people from 9 main sectors in 26 countries in 2016, 32% of the companies working in the aviation, space, defense, and security sectors have provided large digitization in the current situation.

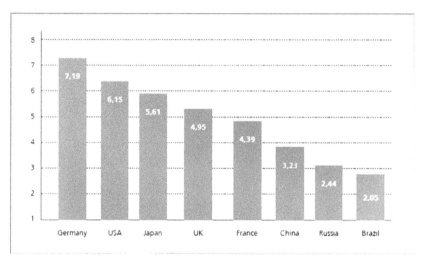

Figure 6. Most Advance Countries in Industry 4.0
Source: (China-Industry 4.0 Index, 2015)

Within 5 years, 76% of these companies are predicted to be digitized. That would amount to about 3.3 percent of the country's yearly turnover (PwC, 2014). The study puts forth three drivers for the above-mentioned investment volume:

1. increased capacity to control horizontal and vertical value chains (productivity improvements by more than 18 percent over the next five years);

2. the increasing digitization and networking of a company's products and services will contribute to ensuring competitiveness, leading to an expected increase in annual sales of 2–3 percent on average or €30 billion per year;

3. new business models are arising from increased cooperation over the entire value chain as well as the integrated use and analysis of data that allow for the satisfaction of even the most individual customer needs (Social Innovation Policy for Industry 4.0, 2017).

What do these developments have in store for people and society? Let us begin with the world of work. Today, the following trends are already emerging:

1. The organization of work is becoming more flexible regarding time and space.

2. Work processes are ever more digitized, more decentralized and less hierarchic.

3. Work processes are becoming more transparent.

4. Ever more routine activities are digitized and automated.

So far in the public discourse, it is rather the progressive and disruptive perspectives on Industry 4.0 that seem to have prevailed, touting above all the opportunities – while the impacts on the labor market are controversial. The anxious question is: Will increasing digitization reduce the number of jobs in manufacturing? There is no definitive answer to this question at the moment. The estimates are too uncertain and differ widely (Social Innovation Policy for Industry 4.0, 2017).

At least one finding has already prevailed. Contrary to the discussions of the 1980s, today it is no longer about human versus machine. Rather, most of the scenarios revolve around a more complex relationship between humans and machines:

1. The automation scenario: systems direct humans. Monitoring and control tasks are taken over by technology. It prepares and distributes information in real time. Employees respond to the needs of cyber-physical systems (CPS) and take on primarily executive tasks. The abilities of lesser skilled workers are thereby devalued.

2. The hybrid scenario: monitoring and control tasks are performed via cooperative and interactive technologies, networked objects and people. The demands on employees increase because they have to be considerably more flexible.

3. The specialization scenario: people use systems. CPS is a tool to support decision-making. The dominant role of the qualified workers is maintained (Social Innovation Policy for Industry 4.0, 2017).

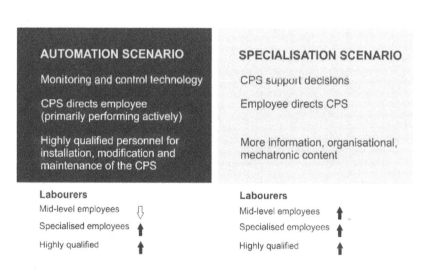

Figure 7. Most Advance Countries in Industry 4.0
Source: (Social Innovation Policy for Industry 4.0, 2017)

Table 1. Opportunities for growth with Industry 4.0
Source: (Social Innovation Policy for Industry 4.0, 2017)

Economic Sectors	Gross added value (billions of euros)		Potential from Industry 4.0	Annual increase	Increase (billions of euros)
	2013	2025	2013-25	2013-25	2013-25
Chemical industry	40,08	52,10	+30,0%	2,21%	12,02
Motor vehicles and automatic parts	74,00	88,80	+20,0%	1,53%	14,80
Machinery and facility engineering	76,79	99,83	+30,0%	2,21%	23,04
Electrical equipment	40,72	52,35	+30,0%	2,21%	12,08
Agriculture and forestry	18,55	21,33	+15,0%	1,17%	2,78
Information and communication technology	93,65	107,70	+15,0%	1,17%	15,04
Joint potential of the 6 selected branches	343,34	422,10	+23,0%	1,74%	78,77
Exemplary extrapolation for the total gross added value in Germany	2.326,61	5.593,06	+11,5,0%	1,27%	267,45

Industry 4.0 also targets some processes. These processes include digitalization and integration of vertical and horizontal value chains, digitalization of product and service requests, digitalization of business models and customer access.

Digitalization and integration of vertical and horizontal value chains: Smart Factories have the flexibility to adapt themselves to a new situation automatically.

People, machinery, and resources in smart factories are modeled in the digital environment and the cyber is in constant communication with the physical environment.

Digitalization of product and service requests: It is possible to obtain data from intelligent products both during production and use.

Digitalization of business models and customer access: Value chain integration with customers and subcontractors (Global Industry 4.0 Survey – Industry key finding, 2016).

2.5. Technologistics

In recent years, technological developments have led to radical changes in all processes ranging from supply management to production management, from distribution management to customer relationship management, from after-sales service management to reverse logistics. This situation also changes the competition style of countries.

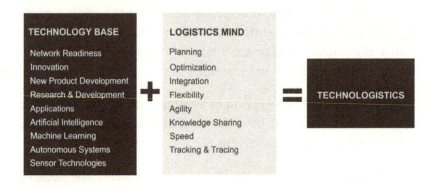

Figure 8. Components of Technologistics

Now, as countries compete, they have started to use factors such as technology, innovation, and speed rather than factors such as product, quality, and price. Firms have understood that production processes which involve technological knowledge or logistic thinking cannot be sufficiently successful separately. Therefore, in today's competitive landscape it is necessary for firms and countries to achieve competitive advantage by evolving a new consciousness, bringing together technological knowledge and logistical insight. The name of this consciousness is Technologistics.

Technologistics is a consciousness that provides a sustainable competitive advantage and advanced company performance to firms that add technological base and logistical thinking to management and operation processes. Firms that act with this consciousness are called Technologistics Firms. In the future, technologistics firms will not only compete but also determine the competition. Countries will take competitive advantage if they develop policies and strategies to acquire Technologistics consciousness.

3. Dynamics of the Internet Age

There is a strong relationship between knowledge and technology. Throughout history, drastic technological developments have followed periods of scientific enlightenment, and technological developments have triggered new periods of scientific enlightenment by facilitating access to information. To understand the current digital divide, it is helpful to review the gradual development of the information revolution. The first wave was the invention of printing press. Thanks to its invention, information has been spread to more people, and the information asymmetry among them has diminished. The second wave was the invention of the steam engine, the industrial revolution and the widespread introduction of transport vehicles. As means of transport became more widespread, interaction among people increased. The third wave began with the global spread of communication technologies. The fourth wave is the internet or hypertext revolution; it is based on the logic of making a connection with the documents.

Regarding access to information today, there are essential differences among individuals who do and do not have access to the internet. This is a serious threat to societies that have not yet fully completed the first stage of the information revolution. There is a risk that their gap with the more developed countries could become unbridgeable.

Digital divides can be identified as 1) the unequal distribution of technological infrastructure usage within a society and 2) the inequality of the rate of technological aptitude throughout that society. The unequal distribution of technological infrastructure is usually a problem of developing countries, while the technological aptitude imbalance within a society is a phenomenon also visible in developed countries, depending on the proportion of young and entrepreneurial populations. A third form of the digital divide is the gap between emerging and developed countries due to their technology usage rates. Measurement of the digital divide between countries is easier than the first two.

The digital divide within the developed world creates inequality of living standards and income throughout the society. As the electronic signature becomes widespread, important developments in the internet trigger economic and social transformations. These developments are happening in the field of trade; the business processing based on paper is rapidly becoming history.

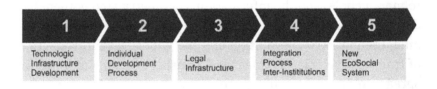

Figure 9. Digital Development Model

Digital development begins with the establishment of the technological infrastructure. Individual development processes follow the establishment of the technological infrastructure. Individual development starts with the increase in personal computer (PC) penetration and continues with the increase in internet penetration. The rise in daily internet usage is one of the most important indicators of the individual development process. With increasing use of the internet, legal infrastructure related to the internet has begun to emerge as well. The most prominent features of these legal developments are based on certain sources: customs, scientific literature, existing laws, and court decisions and case law. When a new social phenomenon emerges without laws specifically concerning it, disputes that arise among individuals are resolved by consulting other sources. As case law is established over time, the distinctive legal resources of the new phenomenon emerge. In other words, the mechanisms of development involve the derivation of new legal rules from the relations of cases with each other by aligning those decisions with the main rules of law. Law comes from behind by nature. It is unthinkable to adopt a law in mature form for a concept newly introduced to a society before its effective use by individuals. For this reason, the spread of internet usage within the society comes first, and then the legal infrastructure develops as a natural process.

Along with the legal development process, an integration process among institutions is also in progress. Today's electronic business applications experience a great deal of confusion because they are developed to meet the specific needs of corporations, without an overall standard. The chaos of electronic business applications can be eliminated through the integration of systems of corporations that communicate with each other in the electronic environment. To eliminate this chaos in electronic business applications and to make business-to-business (B2B) applications that add real value to inter-organizational processes, the solution is to grant legal validity to the e-documents. Establishment of international standards and recognition of the legal validity of e-documents have vital importance for moving the business processes to the Internet and for the integration and simplification of the processes. The establishment of legal infrastructure together with individual and institutional development processes will initiate transformational processes in society that we call a new ecosocial system.

To better understand the Digital Development Model shown in Figure 3, it is useful to re-emphasize the Digital Divide concept in summary: Digital divide can be defined as the unequal distribution of the use of the technological infrastructure within the society and the inequality in the rate of aptitude for technology use among the community segments.

To better understand this concept, it is instructive to emphasize that there are one billion people in the world who have not made a phone call, not even said "Hello" over the phone. In other words, we can understand how important the concept of the digital divide is when you think that there are people who do not even use the phone in the age of mobile phone and internet and that the number of these people is indeed very high.

On the one hand, a computer user who takes full advantage of modern communication possibilities can use mobile technologies and be instantly informed of changes taking place throughout the world. On the other hand, there is still a class devoid of basic communication facilities such as telephone and television. Such a continually widening information gap between these two classes is called the digital divide. There are two distinct forms of the digital divide:

1. Formed among different classes in the society

2. Formed among different countries in the international arena.

The digital divide in a country can be measured by the following three main criteria:

1. The number of telephone subscribers

2. PC numbers.

3. The number of internet users.

The number of internet users is not alone a sufficient indicator. As mentioned in the digital development model, the last stage of individual development is the increase in the internet usage. The digital development model shows the phases a society passes through to become an information society. As seen from the figure, the first stage is the technological infrastructure.

To start the digital development process, governments must first attach importance to infrastructure investments. It is necessary to deliver telephone cables and base stations to every corner of the country, to launch new communication satellites, etc. The second stage is the individual development process. In this stage, the increase in PC penetration among the population (i.e. the ratio of people having PCs), the increase in the internet penetration (i.e. the number of individuals with internet connection), and finally the increase in the internet usage time of the individuals are very important. In the third stage, the internet should be included in the legal infrastructure of the country.

The development of e-government applications in a country is crucial to the process of integration, which is the fourth stage of the digital development model. For example, if the state does not support e-invoicing, e-customs, etc., it is unlikely that private institutions will initiate these applications with their initiatives. We can evaluate e-government development phases in four basic stages;

1. **Emergence phase:** The first phase of the e-government is the creation of individual web pages for all public institutions and communicating with citizens through these pages.

2. **Integration phase:** In this phase, the services given by all institutions on different portals are clustered into a single portal, and common standards for online services are established among the institutions.

3. **Integration Phase:** At this stage, the use of paper documents will be discontinued at government bodies and all transactions will be carried out via electronic documents. Systems of all government agencies will be linked to a common reference-archive system and a common database, which will end the duplication of records and the re-application of citizens to different institutions for business.

4. Social transformation phase: In this phase, mass education campaigns will be implemented to cover all individuals in the society to prevent the digital divide between the individuals who use the Internet and those within the society who do not.

As a conclusion, all applications to support the digital development process must be made in a balanced manner without deepening the information gap, that is without causing additional digital divide between social segments. Imbalance in access to information will also cause the growth of a gap in income distribution. But unfortunately closing the economic gap between the individuals in the future is much more difficult than closing the information gap. As a social technology, the internet has emerged as an advantage for the developing countries — ensuring that the population adapts quickly to the innovations it brings, given the ratio of the young population to the whole population. The inequality of the rate of suitability to technology use among the individuals is a phenomenon which is also visible in the developed countries depending on the share of young and entrepreneur population. Regarding access to information, there are significant differences between individuals who have and who have not accessed to the internet. Today is the information age, and the internet, which is an information ocean, is the most important tool to becoming integrated with the world.

There is a relationship between income level and internet access. In other words, those who have good economic status can access the information more effectively, and the economic chasm widens as lower-income people cannot access information. The difference in wages per employee between industries operating in the field of information technology and other industries is increasing every year.

Today, robots work in factories; all routines that can be done with computers are left to machines in offices, what will happen in the future? Only a very small number of individuals

46

who have mastered information technology in companies will have the opportunity to work, and all core jobs will be left to the machines. Today, it can be seen that all the stages of production in certain industries are made hands-free.

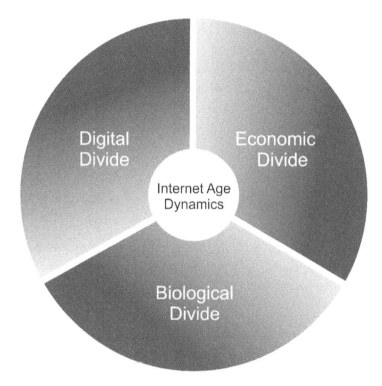

Figure 10. Internet Age Dynamics

The plant workers are usually responsible for maintenance of the machine. The situation is similar in office work. As can be seen in Figure 10, the division between individuals begins with a digital divide resulting from the difference in technology use among individuals, and then develops into an economic divide, as individuals who use technology effectively become economically advantaged. In the future, thanks to the progress of medical developments like stem cell technology, we will see that individuals who

47

are economically strong can look young even in their 70s and have a healthier, higher-quality life. We can call this the biological division. Humanity is moving towards immortality through biotechnical applications and stem cell studies. With cybernetic applications mechanizing people, cyborgs will become real. While, on the one hand, computers are being humanized, on the other, humans are being computerized. The biological divide proposed in the internet age dynamics model can also be associated with different future scenarios. Below are some scenarios of biotechnical and cybernetic applications, which are being put forward or are already taking place:

- The risk of destruction of the food chain by genetically modified plants. Fields cultivated for the production of biodiesel, which is very common today, often grow genetically modified plants.

- With the development of long living possibilities, the proportion of the elderly to the population reaches levels never before experienced in world history, especially in developed countries.

- Parents can choose the characteristics of their children. For example, in China, the rate of female to male birth is on average 100 to 120. (Laws are being enacted against the determination of the gender of the child, seen especially in the Asian countries.)

- Parents may have the opportunity to raise the intelligence of the unborn child, causing the formation of a separate class or even human species over time.

- The biotechnical revolution predicts a longer life and even immortality to the people who are economically strong.

- The emergence of half-human half-machine creatures by the development of cybernetics.

- Use of robots capable of killing against people. Some countries are already carrying out important projects involving robot soldiers in armies.

Why does increasing productivity — that is, doing a lot of work with fewer employees — bring on the crisis, although it is expected to produce products at a lower cost, abundance, and cheapness? Because the people who will consume the products are losing their jobs, and the capital owners of the machines use the profitability from their rising productivity to discount prices to get market share from rivals in the fiercely competitive environment. Therefore, while today's companies are much more productive than the old ones, their profitability has decreased. In this case, companies have to do more work with fewer employees to increase their profitability and to jump ahead of their competitors. This is the reason for the vicious cycle: the customers to whom the companies can sell goods are themselves employees, so demand decreases as unemployment increases.

Today we are locked in this vicious cycle because existing systems cannot respond to this problem. If the capitalist system collapses, the machines owned by capital owners will not work. Communism, once considered as an alternative to capitalism, has already lost its meaning as the working class will be eliminated. In short, an era of new ideologies is looming.

Is there a utopian future where unemployment is a business in the future, where people are paid only because they are citizens, and robots do all work? Or, if the biological divide phase of the Internet's dynamics takes place without system lock-in, will our world be hosting new machine-human creatures?

Could protectionist models, which are now supposed to be a remedy to the crisis, work? Could government expenditures as a tool of state intervention in the economy break today's vicious cycle? This may be realized by the transfer of income from taxpayers to more labor-intensive and inefficient sectors, which taxpayers will oppose, primarily because of claims of the waste of resources. The best example could be the social aids given to low-income families as a palliative measure, and the harsh criticism that these aids are given in an unbalanced way and with political goals. As a result, the inefficient spending of resources will naturally be opposed by the people under the tax burden. Their first aim is to reduce the tax burden on employers and the employee.

But this measure can only delay the problem of unemployment growing due to mechanization. The result will be the age of machines anyway.

In the future, people will be reluctant not only to pay taxes but to pay for any value produced. Today, the film and music industry is struggling with the great chaos created by the internet. Intellectual property rights are essential for the production of quality art and ideas, but protecting these rights on the internet is very difficult.

The Internet economy can be described as a new economic system formed by the increase in productivity and the decrease in costs resulting from the adaptation of Internet technology to classical production systems. It can also be defined as e-everything, because it covers concepts like e-commerce, e-business, and e-government. The basic input to the internet economy is information. In other words, the most important production factor in internet economy is information. In this context, the Internet economy can be seen as the economic consequence of the information age. This result is achieved by technological developments linking individual and society to each other through an electronic nervous system. This electronic nervous system is affecting different parts of the world differently, bringing societies together and establishing a new world order. Briefly:

1. The most important production factor in internet economy is information.

2. The internet economy can be seen as the economic consequence of the information society.

The new world order, which was established as a consequence of globalization and technological developments, has reorganized the forms of business, life, and trade; and today it has created the economic and social system called "Internet Economy." Today, especially in the developed countries, the internet economy system has been more influential on the habits, lifestyles, views, and perceptions of individuals than any economic system before.

The electronic business systems of the future will be the systems that employees and organizations can communicate with at any time from any place. Concepts such as physical office, business hours and holidays will gradually lose their significance and, thanks to the independence of the internet from time, there will be a shift towards business environments that allow employees to work from their homes for 24 hours without having to be in the same physical environment at the same time. These developments show that the empowerment and entrepreneurship of individuals will become more important in the coming years. When the economic effects of the Internet are considered, the phenomenon of globalization needs to be discussed. In essence, globalization refers to the elimination of cultural differences and a tendency towards mono-culturalism among the societies. Today is the information age, and the internet is the most important accelerator of globalization.

Today, making all business processes compatible with the Internet is a prerequisite for competition in the world, and attracting global capital is one of the most important factors determining economic conditions of countries. It has become important to integrate economies with the world's systems as closed economic systems become outdated. This integration can be enabled by the use of compatible systems throughout the world. Internet technologies are evolving at an incredible rate, and electronic signatures that allow legal recognition of transactions on the Internet are beginning to take place all over the world. It can already be foreseen that all foreign trade transactions, which have a prime effect on the competitive power in the global markets, will rapidly move to the electronic environment due to the relative cost advantage, and that paper documents will completely disappear. But it will take time for electronic documents to overtake the dominance of paper documents in business. Two of the reasons are the huge volume of foreign trade transactions and the start-up investments required and their impact on the profitability. There are also great differences between the business processes carried out in the paper environment and those in the paperless environment, and there are a large number of institutions and complex business processes involved in foreign trade transactions.

Competition in global markets becomes tougher day by day, and competition with countries such as China, that can sell goods to world markets at low cost, is becoming more difficult. The operational costs of foreign trade transactions are decreasing as a result of developments in internet technologies in western countries. An era is approaching in which all business processes will be carried out over the internet, and the integration between the institutions will be achieved on a global basis. The second phase of the internet revolution has begun, and there will be dramatic changes in commercial life in the coming years. In this context, companies have a particular obligation to deal with electronic documents at a strategic level. When an electronic document strategy is established, companies need to concentrate primarily on business processes designed to be compatible with electronic documents and to support electronic signatures. It can be said that the most important part of companies' electronic business strategies should be based on electronic documents. All communication inside and outside the company should be done through electronic documents by using an electronic signature, and a very detailed content management system should be established. It is obvious that paper foreign trade documents, which are standard in the field of trade today, will be replaced by electronic documents as the electronic signatures gain legal validity.

The most important indicators showing the level of technological development of a country are the share of research and development expenditures in total expenditures and the share of technology-intensive products in the total exports. Technology is about to reach a level that would bring us to the post-human stage in the evolution. From the 1990's onward, machines have increasingly pushed people out of work. This demonstrates that unemployment will increase all over the world.

4. Basic Electronic Business Models

The concept of electronic business is a broad one. E-commerce is one sub-component of electronic business and an important part. In a broad perspective, electronic business involves the strategic use of information, which is the most important production factor of the new ecosocial system. Electronic business applications increase the effectiveness and efficiency of enterprises by transferring business processes to the electronic environment and thereby enhancing performance. This section focuses on electronic business types.

4.1. e-Business

"Electronic business" means that the operations of the business are transferred to the electronic environment, and that communication with the internal and external environment is carried on in an electronic environment. As "trade" can be defined as the provision of goods or services in return for money, "e-commerce" can be defined as the execution of business processes related to the provision of goods or services via the electronic environment. Accordingly, e-commerce covers only a part of the business process of the enterprise; it is considered a sub-component of electronic business (Laudon & Traver, 2012). Electronic business is a broader concept that can be defined as the way of doing business in the electronic environment. The strategic use of information this makes possible is the most important production factor of the new ecosocial system (Hitt, Ireland, & Hoskisson, 1999).

Today, the strategic use of information requires the transfer of the information exchange — the processes requiring communication

— into the electronic environment. This may involve the automation of communications, as well as faster and more effective realization of communication, both inside and external to the organization, increasing the efficiency of employees. Electronic business
applications increase customer satisfaction and profitability by
shortening business processes. Increasing work efficiency is possible with reduced costs and shorter work processes (Siebel, 2001).

It is essential to transfer all stages of business processes to the
electronic environment with appropriate planning. Since all business processes are interlinked, the use of electronic commerce systems in business requires good planning, organization, and design.
It is necessary to make the accounting system, billing system, logistics facilities, capacity of suppliers, inventory system — in short,
all processes — carried out over the internet. Electronic business
is more than just integrating with suppliers and dealers or building e-commerce sites for end users. Electronic business involves
the exchange of information among employees using the electronic
environment throughout all business processes. That electronic environment is largely considered to be the internet. Today, the internet is the most important channel of information transfer and
management. The internet's importance appears in overcoming
the technological difficulties between institutions using different
electronic communication methods. Such format differences can
be overcome by web based applications (Siebel, 2001).

The internet is also the most effective solution for the inclusion
of suppliers and dealers in rural areas with weak infrastructures
into the electronic business model. The internet provides flexibility for electronic business applications. In the transfer of business
processes — like the supply of raw material, production, inventory,
order, sales, and finance management, advertisement and marketing — into the electronic environment it is crucial that the electronic business system have the flexibility to rapidly harmonize
with changes happening around it. Electronic business systems

should provide the ability to convert, archive, query, analyze and update large volumes of available information. With electronic business applications it becomes possible to control communication both within and outside the enterprise as well as to accelerate all processes related to communication. The goals of electronic business applications include the measurement of the return on marketing and sales activities, the determination of customer profitability, the allocation of enterprise resources by customer profitability, and the supply of products promptly and with appropriate communications.

Measurable benefits of electronic business applications can be summarized as increased revenue, productivity, customer satisfaction and communication quality. Inefficiencies in the procurement process, telephone and fax costs, costs due to high inventory levels, etc., are all reduced through electronic business practices. Clearly, electronic business is a comprehensive concept and is closely related to the vision and corporate culture of the business (Civelek & Sözer, 2003).

Other benefits of electronic business applications include making quick and effective internal and external communication, reducing management costs, making management more effective, minimizing human error, recording all transactions and controlling them more effectively, better evaluating the results of decisions and reducing errors, and increased productivity, profitability and customer satisfaction (Siebel, 2001).

External communication is more difficult to arrange than internal communication. There should be open channels of communication between all the external parties and the organization, and the information transferred must be processed correctly and delivered rapidly to the decision-making mechanisms. Information is an organization's most critical resource. It is important to convert the data collected from its interaction with its external environment into a usable information resource, and to do so quickly. Often the biggest problem when an electronic business model is being established is the absence of a common standard for effective communication. Older forms of information exchange used different channels to communicate with the various people and institutions. Care must be taken to ensure that existing communication channels are not blocked while electronic business models are being created. The new model should be a system that will increase communication among existing channels. As the parties of the new electronic business model harmonize their systems, other communication channels should be gradually deactivated to ensure that communication is maintained through the most efficient channel (Siebel, 2001).

The establishment of an electronic business infrastructure and the implementation of it within the organization are likely to encounter resistance at first. For this reason, it is necessary for the electronic business projects to be supported by intensive training programs and for the top management to be decisive. In the decision-making process, the views of customers in particular, but also those of suppliers, dealers, etc., are all important. One further reason for employee resistance to changes emerging from electronic business applications is the fear that the new system may cause them to lose their jobs (Daft, Management, 1997).

Through electronic communication facilities, raw data gathered from all persons and institutions in communication with the organization must be processed and converted into usable information, and this information must be introduced rapidly into the decision-making mechanisms of the organization without interruption. However, information from all channels will not be in the same format. The electronic business system established for storage and processing of data collected through different communication channels from different electronic communication systems should be compatible with different formats. This transformation of raw data into usable information within the electronic business system is called information management (Shrivastava & Somasundaram, 2009).

Isolated electronic business systems are doomed to fail. It is necessary for the system to integrate with the systems and communication channels used by the persons and institutions with whom organization has external communication. As it is not possible to communicate with all parties via a closed network of common standards, the web-based design of the electronic business system is a good solution. Fast and cost-effective business processes must be implemented for integration. The created system should be designed to adapt to the rapidly changing business environment (Sheldon, 2005).

The properties of good communication infrastructure are summarized below (Civelek & Sözer, 2003):

- Accessibility at anytime from anywhere (with mobile devices or anywhere with internet connection).

- Compatibility with devices manufactured by different manufacturers.

- High system speed.

- System security.

- Continuous running of the system for 24 hours.

- High-capacity help desk and technical service.

- Measurement of the efficiency and performance of the organization by the system.

The concepts of automation and electronic business are often confused. Although automation is an indispensable part of electronic business, it has a different meaning. Electronic business is the use of electronic communication systems to increase and activate business communication and to process information more efficiently in the organization. Automation refers to the elimination of human elements in the business processes and some of the decision-making stages, and to the execution by the system without human involvement (Donaldson, Lae, & Wright, 2012).

The recording, processing, and taking into the decision-making process of complex information can be achieved through the use of electronic business systems. In a world where customers are increasingly demanding, companies need to hurry the migration their business processes to the electronic arena.

Managing knowledge means managing environmental uncertainties, and environmental uncertainty is rapidly increasing in today's business world. This makes information technologies even more important.

Information systems are classified by managerial level: there are administrative information systems and operational information systems. Administrative information systems are the top-level information systems, decision-support systems, and information reporting systems. The operational information systems are the automation systems, transaction record systems, and process control systems (Daft, Management, 1997).

When evaluating the quality of information in electronic business systems, it should be remembered that information should be accessible to the customer any time it is needed and in an updated version. It should also be possible to inquire from the system about the former status of the information and the history of who made the update. In evaluating the quality of information content, the things to be considered are: that the information should be correct, suitable to the user needs and not cover more information than necessary. It is a waste of time to sort out unnecessary information from the necessary. Still, the required information must be complete. The elements of information quality regarding format can be summarized as being easy to understand, presenting a summary and detailed information separately to the user, and including visual, numerical and verbal expressions (Sagawa & Nagano, 2015).

Electronic business systems of the future will be systems that employees and organizations can connect to at any time from any place. Concepts such as physical office, business hours and holidays will gradually lose their significance and, thanks to the independence of the internet from the time of the internet, there will be a shift towards business environments that allow employees to work from their homes without having to inhabit the same physical environment at the same time. As legal validity is granted to the electronic documents, all domestic and foreign trade transactions will begin to be done with them. Likewise, electronic documents will begin to appear in all internal and external communications of organizations, and eventually the use of paper documents will completely disappear. Information systems that are accessible from anywhere and able to operate 24 hours will gradually reduce the dependency on the physical offices. As a result of these developments, companies operating in large offices having a lot of paper documents and files are now being replaced by companies that have settled in small offices that have never used paper, and by those not even settled into an office (Flaherty & Lovato, 2014).

4.2. e-Commerce

Trade can be defined simply as the exchange of money, goods or services between the buyer and seller. In electronic commerce, this exchange is made by using internet technologies. Although the definition of e-commerce includes all electronic means in many different situations, the inclusion of commercial activities that do not use *internet* technologies changes the meaning of the concept. For this reason, the definition of electronic commerce in this study is limited to commercial activities using internet technologies. In this context, although our usage is based on the below definition of "e-commerce" by the Electronic Commerce Coordination Board (ETKK) Legal Working Group, some changes may be proposed in it as well:

"It is a set of commercial transactions carried out with the realization of production, procurement, marketing and sales transactions between legal entities and real persons via computer networks and completion of payment transactions in the same environment (Canpolat, 2001)."

In this definition, there is a limitation such as the completion of payment processes in the same environment, which makes the definition disputable. For example, many processes in B2B and C2C sites are paid out in a different environment. Commercial activities included in the scope of e-commerce are not transactions which started in the electronic environment and also completed in the electronic environment. In a typical B2B transaction, the processes after the meeting of the buyer and the seller are traditionally carried out by using paper documents. This makes the above definition, which is repeated in many sources, a controversial one (Civelek & Sözer, İnternet Ticareti: Yeni EkoSosyal Sistem ve Ticaret Noktaları, 2003). A simpler definition can be proposed as follows:

Electronic commerce is the exchange of money, goods or services between buyer and seller by using internet technology.

Electronic commerce is mainly influential in the production, supply, pricing, competition, and distribution activities of companies. The two most important functions of companies doing trade are production and supply. In today's increasingly competitive environment it is very difficult for companies to maintain their presence. Companies operating in the new ecosocial system have to improve and transform themselves constantly in a brutally competitive environment. Companies that cannot keep up with change and exploit new conditions are doomed to lose their markets. In this context, companies should start to employ technology in all their activities as a way to improve profits in their business. The market chances of companies adopting the electronic business and electronic commerce systems and using these systems efficiently are much higher than companies rejecting these applications (Poirier & Bauer, 2001).

The concept of electronic business is a broader one than electronic commerce. It involves the use of the electronic environment in all business processes within an organization. Electronic commerce is mostly about procurement and sales. Companies that use electronic business systems in production functions can gain significant time and cost savings. Electronic business practices not only save time and costs, they also yield significant gains in product quality. With products manufactured in a shorter time, with better quality and at lower cost, companies can improve their current market position. These positive developments give firms a competitive advantage, allowing them to increase their market shares (Civelek & Sözer, 2003). The use of electronic business and electronic commerce systems in the production and supply processes lowers costs and raises product quality. For example, whereas a company that procures raw materials with traditional methods is forced to work with many intermediaries, a company that uses B2B applications is not required to contact intermediaries and can procure raw material directly from suppliers. Removing the intermediaries within the added-value chain enables those companies to make more efficient procurement. According to the figures given by the OECD, the average difference brought by the intermediaries is 33% above the factory price (OECD, 1999).

Taking this difference into account, companies using electronic business and electronic commerce systems in all supply chain processes may find themselves in an advantageous position in market price competition thanks to the decline in total production costs. In general, when the product sales prices are determined, the costs borne during and after sales should be taken into account, in addition to production and procurement cost items. Examples of these costs include the procurement or rent costs of the physical environment in which the sales activities are carried out, the costs of the procurement operations as well as the cost of after-sale services given to the customers (Civelek & Sözer, 2003).

The costs of procurement or rent that are borne by firms who use classical service methods and sell products through physical stores have reached very high levels. A company that performs part or all of its sales activities via e-commerce applications on the internet is favored with lower costs than a company that trades with traditional methods. Instead of assuming the costs of opening physical stores, it is more strategic to create an online store that is less costly and can be open 24 hours. Electronic commerce applications can also increase sales in the physical environment. A website that provides detailed product information for consumers gives them reasons for going to the physical store and results in saving time in the sales process. E-commerce applications decrease the cost of the human resources, which also has an effect on the product price. Yet, despite all these positive contributions, it should be remembered that, in electronic commerce, each product should be delivered individually to the door of every consumer. This is a serious problem, especially in the sale of low priced products, because the logistic cost per unit increases (Grando & Gosso, 2005) (Civelek & Sözer, 2003).

The literature on electronic commerce enterprises classifies them according to whether buyer and seller is a corporation or an individual. If the buyer and the seller are both corporations, it is called from business to business (B2B). If the buyer is an individual consumer and the seller is a business or corporation it is said to be from business to consumer (B2C). If the buyer and the seller are both individuals, it is called from consumer to consumer (C2C). Electronic commerce is the exchange of money, goods or services between buyer and seller using internet technology at any stage. In addition to the three types mentioned above, there are many websites that fit this definition. This classification is a general classification and does not cover all types of electronic commerce (Laudon & Traver, 2012). Since the scope of this research is the enterprises operating in the field of B2C, it is sufficient to disclose these three types regarding comprehending the difference.

4.2.1. B2B

Electronic commerce which is transacted from business to business is known in the world by the abbreviation "B2B" — which is the initials of the words "Business to Business" in English. In general, it is the name given to the field of e-commerce in which businesses conduct procurement and sales activities by using private or public computer networks.

B2B sites are divided into three groups. The first of these is large-scale B2B sites where all businesses co-exist. The second is the sectoral B2B sites that bring together businesses operating in a particular industry. The third is private B2B sites created by a business for their dealers and suppliers (Yamamoto, 2013).

The private B2B sites are used by an enterprise in the buyer position to perform product procurement, coordination, and communication functions by using a site that is open to suppliers. Such B2B sites are only open to suppliers who are members and closed to others. In this group, no supplier can use the B2B site without the consent of the buyer firm. In the websites of this group, information such as stock status, production planning and product requirements of all companies in the supply chain can be shared simultaneously.

Compared to the B2C, the B2B dates back earlier than the 1990s, before web technologies become widespread. The emergence of Electronic Data Interchange (EDI) applications on wide area networks through computer networks in the 1970s is the first example of an electronic commerce application we call B2B today (Mulligan, 1999). The B2B activities, covering business transactions between enterprises in the field of electronic commerce, play an important role in the total volume of electronic commerce in the world today.

One reason for the high share of B2B transactions in the total volume of e-commerce is that transaction volumes of companies in trade are much higher than the purchasing volumes of individuals. A second reason is the consumer hesitations in B2C transactions, which is actually the subject of this thesis (Laudon & Traver, 2012).

Figure 3 shows the increase in B2B transaction volumes over the years. Despite the fact that B2B applications date back to the 1970s, it was early in the 2000s that the volume of B2B transactions on the internet began to increase, as shown in Figure 3. This is why the worldwide use of EDI applications continues even today. The widespread use of large-scale B2B sites such as Alibaba.com began in the mid-2000s. The EDI system, which emerged in the 1970s, gained an Internet-based feature with the introduction of the Internet in the 1990s. Since then, many companies have started to use the new version of the Internet-based EDI system instead of the traditional EDI system working in wide area networks (Akbay, 2009).

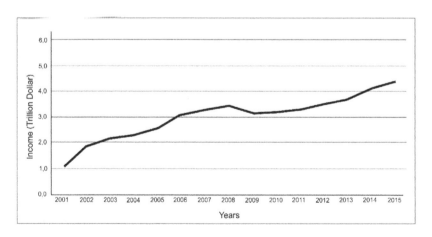

Figure 11. Growth of B2B Volume. Source: (Laudon & Traver, 2012)

Another classification used to define the types of B2B sites is to classify B2B sites according to the target market or industries. According to this classification, there are two groups: vertical and horizontal.

Vertical B2B sites are established to bring together businesses operating in a particular industry. One of the most important features of vertical B2B sites is that they mainly involve conventional industries. For example, eSteel.com was established specifically for the iron and steel sector, fuelquest.com was established for the energy sector, covisint.com was established for the automotive sector, and chematch.com was established for the chemical sector. These are B2B websites established to operate within these industries. Common features of vertical B2B sites are: companies in the supply chain are spread over a wide geography, the chain covers many companies, and business process are complicated. The vertical B2B sites often target industries with a high number of buyers and sellers and wide geographical distribution (Ravichandran, Pant, & Chatterjee, 2007).

In the industries where it is difficult to find customers with classical methods, the use of vertical B2B sites offers significant advantages. Vertical B2B sites are also sensitive to change. For example, e-steel.com, which operates in the iron and steel industry, was established with the aim of reducing the costs of excess inventory in the industry. Some vertical B2B sites target more than one industry. The reason for these types of B2B sites is that often it would not be profitable to the website to operate only in a single industry.

The second group is the horizontal B2B sites. Horizontal B2B sites are those where many industries are together, and different services and products can be bought and sold.

Today's electronic business (e-business) applications have increased internal and external communication in foreign trade companies. The use of Business to Business (B2B) sites such as

Alibaba.com has become widespread worldwide, and the effectiveness of foreign trade companies has increased. However, since the use of electronic formats for documents used in foreign trade has not reached a sufficient level of worldwide acceptance, paper documents are still widely used and are still being sent by courier; their legal validity does not survive when they are transmitted over the internet after conversion into picture files (Pagnoni & Visconti, 2010).

Greater use of electronic documents, however, is rapidly becoming widespread in all business lines. There is a long history of studies carried out for the preparation of electronic versions of documents used in foreign trade, but there are still various reasons why it is not widespread. The growth of the use and acceptance of electronic documents can be the beginning of a new era for B2B sites.

4.2.2. B2C

Electronic commerce from business to consumer is known in the literature as "B2C" — which is an abbreviation of "Business to Customer" e-commerce in English. It is the name given to the field of electronic commerce where the companies perform their marketing, sales and distribution activities to the consumer by using computer networks.

The volume of B2C transactions is rapidly increasing around the world, and this increase is predicted to continue in the coming years. Figure 6 shows the worldwide volume of B2C, including forecast figures prepared in line with the statistics prepared by Goldman Sachs. According to these figures, the world B2C volume reached 752.33 billion dollars by the end of 2014 (Goldman Sachs, 2015). As seen in Figure 6, the increase in B2C volume is predicted to continue unabated. B2C also has a great potential in Turkey, and there are still opportunities for new investors. The development and dimensions of the B2C domain are closely related to the widespread use of internet in the world and the users' perception and adoption of the internet as the field of shopping.

The full-fledged emergence and expansion of B2C applications coincided with the mid-1990s. The Seattle-based company Amazon.com, which began selling books on the internet in 1995, is now at the forefront of B2C success stories.

Since the mid-1990s, many companies have started B2C activities by shifting some sales channels to the internet. The worldwide volume of B2C transactions since the establishment of Amazon.com in 1995 is as seen in Figure 12.

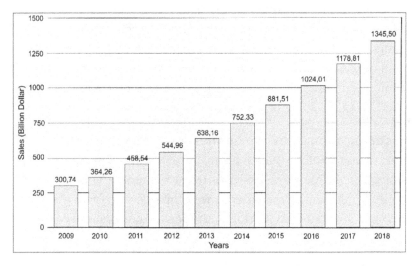

Figure 12. Growth of B2C Volume. Kaynak: (Goldman Sachs, 2015)

When B2C electronic commerce volumes are examined, it is clear that there is a tendency to rise in a relatively straight line from the beginning to the present day, but when the dimensions of that rise are compared with the number of internet users, it is seen that the rate of increase is relatively low.

There are two important reasons for this. The first is consumers' safety concerns. In general, consumers are uncomfortable about sharing credit card information over the internet. The most important hesitancy of consumers regarding credit card purchases over the internet is related to credit card information. Some of these hesitancies include fears of unauthorized use and the selling of customer information due to negligence or misuse by the company. Other reasons involve the use of credit card information by hackers intruding into the transaction between the customers and companies and stealing the information.

The second major consumer hesitancy regarding B2C sites is buying products without seeing and touching them. This concern varies among product types (Khan & Matin, 2004).

4.2.3. C2C

From consumer to consumer electronic commerce is known by the abbreviation C2C — which is the initials of "Consumer to Consumer" in English. In general, this name is given to the field of electronic commerce where the consumers on the internet perform second-hand sales activities among themselves.

The C2C websites first emerged as auction sites. Applications called e-auctions are sites where users can bid for products similar to traditional auctions. Today auction sites are gradually decreasing. The C2C originally gained popularity by e-Bay, which is the world's most famous C2C site (Altaş, 2014). Although usually it is second-hand products that are sold in the C2C websites, first-hand products are sold as well. The sale of first-hand products by individuals without invoicing can be categorized as online vending. First-hand products can also be sold with only an invoice generated by an individual. The term "drop-shipping" is used for this type of sales which means sales without inventory (Chen, Chen, Parlar, & Xiao, 2011).

In this sale type, the individual makes a drop shipping agreement with an enterprise and tries to find customers on C2C sites for its products. After finding the customer and making the sale, it sends the order to the enterprise, and the enterprise sends the product to the customer together with the invoice. The individual who acts as the intermediary in this process receives the commission from the transaction. C2C sites are also known as the ad site. Although these websites are usually defined as those where second-hand products are bought are sold, real estate brokers and car galleries are also operating in C2C websites. In this case, it should be taken into account that the goods are second hand and that the final buyer and seller are individuals (Sonnenberg & Darrow, 2011). Today, C2C sites have important functions in the elimination of information asymmetry between buyer and seller and in the formation of market prices for second-hand products (Dan, 2014).

5. Management of B2C Web Sites

Management and performance management of B2C enterprises are becoming increasingly important. Performance is a multidimensional concept that considers the overall success of the business — that is, the degree to which the objectives of the business are being achieved. The short-term goals of enterprises are to increase the productivity, decrease the inventory level and shorten the turnover period, while the long-term goals are to increase market share and profitability. Financial metrics and market measurement data have been tools used to make comparisons between enterprises and to evaluate the relative position of enterprises over time. The first two concepts that come to mind about performance dimensions in business management are sales and firm size. It is now clear that efficiency and productivity factors should also be added to these two dimensions. Indeed, Drucker draws attention to concepts of efficiency and productivity by arguing that performance is composed of two important dimensions. These are: effectiveness, or is rate at which a firm performs the specified objectives; and efficiency, the achievement of desired outputs with minimum resource outlay (raw material, capital, human resource). Enterprise performance can thus be defined as the achievement of enterprise objectives with an efficient and effective manner (Daft, Management, 1997) (Perotin & Robinson, 2004).

In fact, the definition of (good) management is the efficient and effective fulfillment of business objectives. This definition overlaps with that of performance. In industrialized societies driven by complex technologies, organizations are social systems assembling

71

information, people, and raw materials to perform a task. If these social systems are structured for profit, they are called enterprises. From this definition's perspective, the responsibility of the manager is to organize the resources the enterprise possesses in order to realize the business objectives efficiently and effectively (Daft, Management, 1997).

In the literature, various measurement criteria are used to measure business performance, such as return on investment (ROI), market share, the profit margin on sales, ROI growth rate, increase in sales, increase in market share and competitive position. In the 2000s, it can be said that new dimensions — such as benefitting from inputs, quality and innovation — are now added to these factors, and the scope of the concept of performance has been expanded. Today, it is observed that dimensions of employee behavior, market share, product or market leadership, and social responsibility are also added to this classification (Çemberci, 2012).

The enterprise performance also implies the responsibilities of the organization to the stakeholders. A company's achievement of its profit target in an efficient and effective way would mean that it is fulfilling the responsibilities to the stakeholders. However, measuring the enterprise performance only through profitability and cost is taking a very narrow perspective, because the most important factors providing competitive advantage against rivals in today's competitive environment are not just sales and firm size. Business performance is fully expressed when evaluated in conjunction with sales, business size, efficiency, and effectiveness. For this reason, when dimensions of enterprise performance are all considered together, it consists of sales, business size, efficiency and efficiency (Harrison & Wicks, 2013).

In addition to these dimensions, which are used to determine the numerical status of the enterprise performance, there are also key factors that influence the shape, direction, and size of the performance. These key factors focus on information and information management, which are the most important requirements of the age we live in. Focusing on these factors will enable businesses to achieve long-term sustainable enterprise performance rather than short-term performance (Civelek, Çemberci, Kibritci Artar, & Uca, 2015).

Sustainable business performance is one of the most frequently encountered problems faced by firms in today's competitive environment. Changes in consumer needs from day to day, geographical shifts in labor, new products, and market development efforts do not allow the commercial activities of the world to be carried out in routine processes. It is extremely difficult to standardize competitors, customers and the marketplace around a competition framework where a product ordered from Europe is managed in America and produced in Africa (Baaij & Greenven, 2004).

In a business environment where competition can be quite ruthless, competitive advantage can only be created by incorporating some information in production processes that cannot be easily imitated and which is specific to the company. Companies that include unique types of information in their production processes cannot be easily imitated by their competitors, and they will have a say in the market by offering different and unique products to customers. Enterprises can easily be imitated by their competitors unless they add distinctive and non-imitable information to the production process. Creating and managing information both on management and production subjects, from production processes to ways of doing business, from marketing strategies to human resources management, will become the most important determinants of sustainable business performance (Civelek, Çemberci, Kibritci Artar, & Uca, 2015).

When the classical production factors such as labor, capital, and nature are considered in regard to the value added to the enterprise, in today's highly competitive environment their importance seems to decrease gradually. In the industries where information technology is heavily used, the role of labor in creating added value is gradually falling, and surprisingly, capital becomes insignificant compared to the value created. For example, the world-famous social network giant Facebook, which has reached a company value of $ 250 billion, has a relatively low start-up capital (Davis, 2015). And at the same time, the share of labor in this value is quite low when compared to other sectors. From these examples, we can argue that where new production factors are introduced in the new ecosocial system, the classical production factors gradually lose their influence and importance. The most important of these new production factors is information. It is the production factor that creates the most added value today. So for this reason, the concept of knowledge management has become the most important element in determining the performance of firms (Chuang, Liao, & Lin, 2013).

Today, information management systems are the most important factors impacting business performance. The most important element for companies operating in the field of business-to-customer electronic commerce is the website. The success of the website is the single most important ingredient affecting the performance of the enterprise. The most important factor that determines the success of a website is the customers' preference for the site over other competing sites. It is a natural result that B2C sites have low performance when the performance of the website is low because all processes such as ordering, payment, follow-up, customer relations are carried out through the website. Therefore, the website performance for B2C sites is directly related to enterprise performance. The website's ability to meet customer expectations and even provide services beyond expectations will positively impact enterprise performance.

The determinants of the website's performance are the quality of service, quality of information and quality of the system. The quality of the information relates to the information which can be accessed via a specific website. It is about whether the site meets the expectation of the user regarding the quality of the information. The quality of the system is about the intelligibility of the system, ease of learning how it works, simple surfing among menus as well as quick working and with no hanging and crashing. Service quality refers to the reputation of a website, the trust it gives to the consumer, and the quality of the communication it has established with the user. The quality of service is related to the user's confidence that the personal information entered on the site will not be used for malign purposes, the feeling of customization given by the website to the users, and easy communication with the site management (Chen, Rungruengsamrit, Rajkumar, & Yen, 2013). These factors together constitute the performance of the website and indirectly determine the performance of the enterprise.

6. Post-Digital EcoSystems

I am sure that when we all see photos from years before, we think that ourselves and our friends look different and strange. When we see our clothes, our body, our facial expressions and even our facial lines, we say "Did I really look like this? I cannot believe myself ... ". The older the photo, the greater your astonishment. Sometimes we do not even want to put those old photos anywhere they could be seen. At least we do not want anyone outside of our immediate vicinity to see them. Everything that was very fashionable in those days would be reflected in that photograph... We feel those days in the photo with the hairstyle, clothes, and places or briefly that period, but all these features that we like that day are "outdated" from today's window. Clothes, shoes, watches, furniture, home appliances, music, TV productions, and relationships are all outdated. Humanity changes, everything in his life follows this change. As a result, the only thing that does not change is the change itself ...

When you put your pictures taken in two different periods side by side, finding ten basic similarities between these two pictures is more difficult than finding ten basic differences. Change is now happening faster than ever before. People are beginning to consume their production faster. In the past, the clothes were worn longer; TV series lasted longer, music albums played longer. The consumption period of many elements of our lives has now been reduced. The main reason for this particular change is the technology-driven process of individual and social development, starting from the 1980s and continuing today at an unbelievable pace. In our publication "Internet Ticareti" dated 2003, we mentioned the formation of a New Ecosocial System (NES) as a result of this development process. We have defined this new system as "an economic and social system that is constantly renewing and covering new communication, business, commerce, and lifestyles, resulting from technological developments linking societies living in the world with an electronic nervous system in the national and international arena."

Individuals who complete the process of development and who change with the new system, acquire the characteristics of information-society individuals; in other words, they become well-informed, competent, social, investigating, innovative, and open to development, and they also become customers who demand quality products and customized service. The detailed information profiles of today's consumers naturally affect the market strategies of today's companies and their approaches to customers. "Change" at the organizational and individual level is now viewed as a management problem. Corporations are getting assistance from change manager professionals to adapt their organizations, business processes, and employees to new market dynamics. Corporations that cannot complete this change process find it difficult to adapt to new market dynamics; and these companies are poised to risk losing their markets.

Albert Einstein's phrase fully fits this era: "Life is like riding a bicycle. To keep your balance, you must keep moving." The political, social and economic implications of the rapid development, change and transformation process we live in are experienced instantly due to narrowing of the impact response frequency range, like an accelerating karma. This means that to be able to sustain their market shares and become successful, companies must replace their old static organizational structures with fast-responding structures and get aligned with new market norms in strategic and tactical layers.

There are three main dynamics marking this era, which we can define as the post-digital era for the business world: transformational innovation, the neo-customer, and social interaction.

6.1. Transformational Innovation

Transformational innovation — or the disruption of existing ecosystems by addressing customer desires with a new technology-supported business model — will continue to be the most important game changer in the post-digital era. Regardless of industry, companies that have been market leaders for decades can be taken down by new companies who can emerge at any time. Competitive advantage is no longer permanent or even sustainable in the long-term, and competitors can take away customers at any time. One famous example of such innovation, Uber has begun to show the devastating effect on traditional companies, not as a new taxi company, but as a new business model that changes the way taxis are used. In the post-digital era, examples like Uber, Airbnb, Net-Flix, etc. are expected to grow and become more popular.

6.2. Neo-Customers

In the post-digital period, we see the power of the company sliding into the hands of the customers. No matter the generation, these neo-consumers have consumer characteristics that transform them from need-oriented individuals to demand-oriented customers. They have more demands, less time to spend, limited attention, and have easily affected and shorter customer journeys.

Neo-customers are currently so divided in their traditional customer segments that they cannot be grouped regarding their desires and preferences. But they have similar characteristics in consumer behavior codes, and they will trigger high competition in the post-digital era where online and offline markets are equipped with multichannel, vast alternatives.

6.3. Social Interaction

These neo-customers should be regarded by companies not only as individuals who use their products and services but also as reference points who may transfer their first-hand experiences about brands to the larger market audience.

As we all experience, neo-customers take greater account of the messages given by reference points like the near environment, other customers, and subject experts than they do of the communications of the media bought by companies. It should be noted that in a consumer ecosystem that is hyperlinked in digital ways, while neo-consumer sharing can be a source of near-infinite competitive advantage for a brand, it also includes risks arising from essential massive reactions.

An episode of the visionary technology series Black Mirror describes a social order that is based on the online ranking of individuals about each other, following their online and offline interaction. In this society, class relationships, basic rights, and even freedoms are linked to the ranking system. It is important to note that, for now, this possible social order in the future applies to companies, not to individuals. It will be seen that in the post-digital period companies with low social rankings stemming from poor social interactions will have little chance to survive and that the effect of social interaction on consumer purchasing decisions will continue to increase.

7. Strategies in Post-Digital Ecosystems

7.1. First Strategy: Unique Customer Experience Design

The common feature of successful brands in the post-digital era will be the strategic and tactical adaptation to these new dynamics to create a sustainable, unique customer experience that is essential for leadership in their industry. The customer experience — which we can define as the sum of all the interactions of a customer with the brand — is the coming together of multiple micro-experiences: the interactions between the customer and the brand and the emergence of a brand reception and value in the customer. The post-digital era will set the stage for the rivalry of companies competing to give their customers a unique experience on their journey with their brands. During this period, customers will demand that brands meet, or go even beyond, their expectations consistently and continuously in a real-time relationship having multi-channels and more than one connection point. Brands that achieve this with a sustainable and unique customer experience will gain a lasting competitive advantage.

To create a sustainable and unique customer experience, it is necessary to create a strategic and tactical infrastructure from the top down at the whole company level and with a holistic approach. Therefore, sustainable and unique customer experience should be planned, created and managed strategically and tactically in two layers.

7.1.1. Strategic Customer Experience Layer

Strategically, infrastructure needs to be available at three key points: Organizational culture, insight system and customer focus.

7.1.1.1. Organizational Culture

The structure and content of the company's operation and approach cultures emerge as important factors in the financial performance of the brand in the post-digital period. Companies that move with top-down common sense towards the objective of offering unique customer experience will get better financial results than companies that focus on increasing sales figures with short-term planning. To achieve these objectives, not only the marketing department, but also the human resources, accounting, IT, and all other units need to establish a synergy-based organization with a system that allows them to act within the infrastructure and have a shared responsibility to fulfill their missions in the design of a unique customer experience.

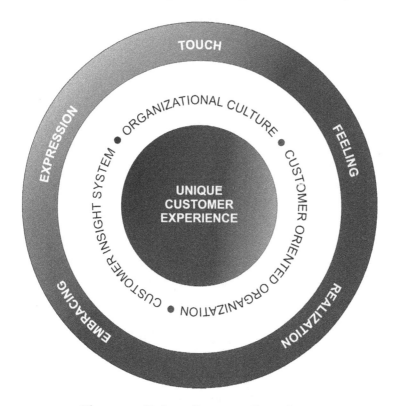

Figure 13. Unique Customer Experience

Unfortunately, a fairly low proportion of companies competing in the market have been able to incorporate into the process business units such as IT and Human Resources that play important parts in customer experience, and few have created participatory corporate cultures or organizations. The importance of internal customer experience in creating customer experience strategies is quite obvious. As an employer brand, the company needs to create conditions that will create a unique customer experience for its employees, which are the internal customers, and this should be reflected to the external customers. It would be optimistic (and foolish) to expect an organization with disgruntled employees to create customer interactions providing a positive, innovative, and unique customer experience. In conclusion, organizational infrastructure and culture must be ready to contribute to this unique customer experience.

7.1.1.2. Customer Insight System

As we all know, in the business world there are balances within each period. Thirty or forty years ago it was possible to recognize customers and follow their behavior only at a macro level. There were no behavioral codes for customers at that time, but these are available today. Companies reached less well-known customers with a product and sales oriented marketing approach. In the post-digital era, it is necessary to reach customers with a more personalized and experience-oriented marketing approach, even though companies now have a data flow that can be monitored and tracked for every move of the customer. Hence, each period creates its reality, or in other words, prophecy fulfills itself. One of the infrastructures required to plan unique customer experience in the post-digital period an insight system, that is, an organizational structure that will recognize the customer, and more importantly, understand what she wants and produce results accordingly. Successful companies need to establish the insight systems strategically and to use them effectively throughout the organization. Creating an innovative business model infrastructure with the help of technology is, in fact, quite easy; what is indeed difficult is to find out on what innovation should be done. Similarly, designing customer experience at an operational level is an easy part of the job, and what matters is understanding what customers like or do not like, or exactly what they want. To overcome these sorts of difficulties, it is necessary to establish an insight business unit within the organization; a unit which works independently to form a collective organizational skill infrastructure within the corporation and ensures coordination between the different business units. This function must be responsible for analyzing customer data from multiple channels by using collective organizational skills, integrating these data with creative approaches and transforming them into customer insights that enable the creation of a unique customer experience and thus into effective marketing strategies and tactics.

7.1.1.3. Customer Oriented Organization

The creation of a customer-focused mindset is one of the strategic prerequisites for the company trying to create a unique customer experience. We can define the concept of customer orientation as the approach that is aimed primarily at placing the customer at the heart of the organization. Customer orientation creates a dynamic, proactive, fast and steadily evolving organization that will maximize the value that the customer will gain during this journey. In the post-digital era, traditional demographic or RFM-style segments have begun to be replaced by singular customers and their profiles, now forming a single segment. To achieve a true and effective customer experience, the customer should be at the heart of the organization while there should be a multi-channel, real-time system around the customer and this system should be encircled by the products and services of the brand. Accordingly, the entire ecosystem of the company needs to be organized to put the customer at the focus. Customer-focused thinking of business partners, vendors, dealers, service providers, suppliers and all other stakeholders is one of the most critical factors for successful strategic implementation. It is inevitable that the brand will be damaged if the after-sales services do not meet customer expectations. Therefore, in comparison with rivals, companies that establish a customer-focused organizational ecosystem will be closer to delivering unique customer experiences and thereby will obtain a sustainable competitive advantage, thanks to the maximum value perception created during the customer's journey.

7.1.2. Tactical Customer Experience Layer

The development of a strategic infrastructure in the post-digital era is not by itself sufficient to create a sustainable, unique customer experience. Five tactical approaches need to be applied holistically to determine and achieve strategic goals by using this infrastructure. These approaches are listed as Expression, Touch, Feeling, Realization, and Embracing, respectively.

7.1.2.1. Expression

To reach persuasively into the minds of neo-customers looking for reality, sincerity, and honesty, it is necessary to transfer a brand's missions to its potential customers and to build social partnerships with them. First of all, brands need to give their potential customers rational reasons to choose them. The most important tool for this is a well-designed corporate mission. This mission needs to include outward and collective benefits rather than a few inward commercial objectives. For example, Apple's mission is "being committed to bringing the best personal computing experience to students, educators, creative professionals and consumers around the world through its innovative hardware, software and Internet offerings." Facebook has built its mission as "giving people the power to share and making the world more open and connected." As it can be seen, their mission statements did not include inward messages aimed at the company or its shareholders but outward messages about what their activities provide to society.

In the post-digital era, consumers want to see more than a simple commercial-minded merchant. Although it is evident that the basic motivation of a company is to create the maximum financial value for all its shareholders, what is expected in the post-digital era is to return some of that value to society, i.e. to the consumers, vendors, business partners and rest of the society. In general, social responsibility programs that are attempted without links to the brand's social purpose and its contribution to its field of operation are ineffective in the post-digital era; neo-customers can form a skeptical perception of the sincerity of such incongruent programs. The main motivation of such communication activities may still be commercially oriented, and the brand may be far from sincere. In the post-digital era, creating a customer journey designed with a social partnership component in which the customers express their objectives makes the customer a shareholder of such objectives and helps the brand to achieve success. Therefore, in the creation of the unique customer experience, the important factors are a brand's explanation of its social goals, the benefits it offers to society, and its means for doing so — in honest, transparent, and realistic communication methods — and the neo-customers' internalization of those rational and emotional reasons for the use of the brand.

7.1.2.2. Touch

A bi-directional physical interaction between the brand and the neo-customer is one of the most important factors that influence the customer experience. In the post-digital era, customers have the opportunity to interact with the brand whenever they want and through whatever means they want in a multi-channel communication environment, and they expect this flexibility from the brands as a standard customer service. It is not enough that brand and customer interaction is now on-line, real-time interaction appears to be a very important customer expectation as well. On the other side, for brands to create a positive experience, they need to serve customers from the right channel, at the right time, with the right product and the right message. To achieve this, there is a need for technical and organizational infrastructure where customer insight systems work effectively. Thanks to these infrastructures prepared in the strategic layer, during their interactions in a single or in different channels for each customer, service by the companies delivered at the same consistently high level is vital in terms of creating a unique customer experience.

7.1.2.3. Feeling

The most important factor influencing the customer experience in the tactical layer is the feeling awakened in the customer after each interaction. The brand's communication needs to provoke the desired emotions in the customer as a result of every interaction between them. To create a unique customer experience, every interaction of the customer with the brand needs to ensure the arousal of the target feelings to the customer. In the post-digital period, the interactions which do not awaken feelings remains shallow and more vulnerable to threats from competition.

7.1.2.4. Realization

Neo-customers want to see that products and services delivered to them at every step of their journey through the brand, before, during, and after purchase, with specific minimum standards for quality and service. If the tablet computer produced and sold by the company is inefficient due to hardware failure, the company will not be preferred due to that inefficiency, even if the brand is a customer-oriented company.

In the post-digital period, some variables in the price and benefit equation, such as product properties, have become less weighty. Instead, customer experience has become the single factor with the highest weight in the equation. Therefore, in order to avoid customer experiences that create competitive disadvantage, it is necessary to ensure that the products and services are designed to meet all expectations of the customers and that the customers in turn are satisfied with the performance of the products and services.

7.1.2.5. Embracing

Another tactical factor that makes the customer's experience with the brand more meaningful and naturally extends his journey with the brand is the creation of an environment that provides the customer with a feeling of ownership and belonging. At this point, it is also important to set up platforms where customers who prefer the brand can share their experiences and act as brand ambassadors. As in the case of Harley-Davidson, brand associations emerge as a result of bringing consumers together; they meet in a common lifestyle denominator even if they have different backgrounds and preferences. Such programs can have a great positive impact on customer experience. Therefore, brands that aim to create a unique customer experience need to apply programs that support consumers participation in brand communities, which become their social common denominators.

In conclusion, to achieve sustainable competitive advantage in the post-digital era, companies need to create strategic and tactical infrastructures and give their customers unique experiences through their brands. In this period, especially when the life cycle of brands is very short, customer experience has become a basic requirement, not a luxury, for companies to stay competitive. All companies need to pay attention and create roadmaps in this direction.

7.2. Second Strategy: Customer Journey Engineering

The fact that the market value of Tesla, the manufacturer of electric cars, is competing with that of 100-year-old automotive giant Ford, clearly demonstrates the asymmetric ecosystem we now find ourselves living in. Although it does not have satisfactory production figures, let alone sales, and shows losses every year, the perception of Tesla is as a technology company, while Ford, in the same industry, is perceived as traditional industry company. This demonstrates the effect on the market value of the company that the perception of technology and vision can have in a short period.

While we started to live with new habits in an old town, Tesla and the other examples show us that the town has also started to change. As the new rules become valid in our changing town, to survive and to compete, it is becoming a necessity for companies to comply with this new rule. The marketing ecosystem, which is a part of the whole, is taking its share of this change and transformation.

7.2.1. The Transformation of Marketing Eco-System from Vertical to Horizontal

The most important factor in the transformation of the marketing ecosystem is the connection of consumers to each other. The collective power created by connected consumers has led to structural changes in the marketing ecosystem as well as a transformation of the ecosystem from Vertical to Horizontal. In other words, the vertical flow directly towards the consumer from the company has given way to horizontal processes involving consumer-dominant product development, communication and customer relations.

7.2.1.1. Customers as the Innovation and Product Development Partners

Product development and innovation processes are no longer taking place vertically from companies to the market but rather in horizontal structure with the participation of consumers. The most important factor in companies' creation of successful products and services is the development of joint projects with consumers that make them the focal point of the process. In this context, companies that catch the day are switching from research-based product development models to joint development models based on the connection with the user. Crowd-sourcing is one of the natural consequences of this transformation. Company research findings show the value of information from the customer and that products developed by crowd-sourcing have a positive impact on sales performance.

7.2.1.2. Customers as New Media Channel

From the communication perspective, the traditional model of communication from the brand-to-customer in a vertical structure has begun to evolve towards a consumer-to-consumer model. Although the neo-consumer profiles are connected and available at all times, their distracted and hearing-but-not-listening moods make it difficult for brands to effectively deliver value proposals to the target audience. A recent study by the US National Center for Biotechnology Information confirms that consumers' attention spans shrank from 12 seconds in 2000 to 8 seconds in 2013. In younger generations, this period goes down further. The one-way and company-to-consumer communication model in the vertical structure, which has begun to lose its effectiveness, has given way to a consumer-to-consumer horizontal structure, and the control of communication has passed from the brands to the consumers, who have started to function as a media channel.

7.2.1.3. Customers as Reference Sources

Regarding customer relations management, one of the most important factors influencing neo-consumers' brand preferences is trust. In today's markets, minimum standards for products and services are established, and no brands that offer values below these standards can compete. The sense of trust that brands had established vertically in the previous era through marketing communication is now established in a predominantly horizontal structure through interaction between consumers. Therefore, the weight of social references has gained importance in the decision mechanism of consumers. Business models supported by natural, genuine and sincere approaches from companies towards their

STRATEGIC EXCELLENCE IN POST-DIGITAL ECOSYSTEMS

customers — and in which they consider customers as social partners — appear to be main features of winning brands.

In conclusion, the competitiveness of brands in the new period is determined not by their financial size and their past but by their integration with consumer communities.

7.2.2. The Focusing on Architecture of Customer Journey for Success

As long as customers' expectations are met, they continue their journey with the brand. The higher the perceived value in this journey, the more likely it is for customers to move to the level of brand advocacy. For the company to reach this ultimate goal, all the leaders in the organization, especially the marketing managers, should accompany the customers on their journeys with the brand — to facilitate the path and enable the customer to continue the journey smoothly and with a perception of high value.

For the realization of strategic objectives, the customer journey architecture needs to support these goals effectively. At this point, three basic approaches need to be established and adopted by the whole corporation.

7.2.2.1. Customers as the Most Valuable Assets of Organizations

One of the first perspectives necessary for companies that want to realize their strategic goals is to consider their customers as the most valuable asset on the company's balance sheet. The Basic Performance Indicators that this will be form need to be designed to reflect the quantity, volume and value changes in the customer portfolio. In this context, three key performance criteria should be established, and the company targets should be determined within the framework of these criteria.

First of all, while each company gains new customers on one

hand, it loses some of its current portfolio of customers for various reasons on the other. The ideal situation is gaining new customers without losing any old ones, but in practice this is not possible. Marketing and sales managers often try to establish a gained and lost customer quantity-based balance, ignoring the customer value-based balance which is more important. In targeted works, planning should be done in such a way that the total potential value contributions (lifetime value) of the gained customers should compensate and even exceed the total value loss of the lost customer portfolio. Without careful planning there may be a risk of decline in total customer asset value, even if the company has a high retention rate. In consequence, it is necessary to move beyond this quantity-based perspective to prevent declines in the total customer value, which is the company's most valuable asset.

Secondly, while customer losses are natural in competition, and those losses are offset by gains in the total customer value, it is still necessary to identify the reasons behind customer losses, to reduce the loss rate, and to increase the value-based retention rate. When these reasons are determined, it is then necessary to take measures to regain the lost customers and to prevent loss of the existing customers over these reasons. Consequently, the rate of customers regained and the retention rates of existing customers should be included in the performance indicator tables as an important key performance criterion.

Thirdly, companies that set targets and act to improve their total customer asset values must focus on Net Customer Value Gain/ Loss, calculated over the results of these objectives. The Net Customer Value Gain/Loss is calculated by subtracting the total asset values of the lost from the gained customers, and it is the most important key performance criterion to support customer-focused growth (Bliss, 2015).

7.2.2.2. Customers as Building Blocks of Total Experience

For strategic objectives to be realized, the customer journey should be the main focus of the organization, and every step of this journey should be optimized to maximize customer experience. When she buys goods or services, each customer interacts with the company in multiple stages and through different contact points. From the first meeting with the brand, to getting information and deals offered, to making an evaluation, through the purchasing and after-sales process, customer objectives and motivations can be different. This process, from one end to the other, forms the journey of the customer with the brand, and, regarding the realization of the strategic goals for the companies, it is important to make the journey as long as possible as this increases the customer's lifetime value contribution.

In this end-to-end journey, companies should not name the stages of the journey according to their internal processes, but name them rather by matching the expectation, needs, and perspective of the customer. For example, while the customer to whom the offer is given, is perceived as a potential target for the company, from the customer's viewpoint the offer is the start of an important process for meeting their need, a step towards forming a short assessment list, and a critical period before the final decision.

All the leaders in the organization and all the business units affiliated with these leaders should look at every stage of the journey through the eyes of the customer and as part of total experience. At the end of each stage they need to have reached a level of experience that will give customers clear and positive answers to four critical issues. In this context, customers need to be able to confirm that their goals are realized at the end of the relevant phase, to define what they have achieved, to declare their intent to continue their interactions, and to convey the experience to other consumers.

For the customer experience to achieve a level that ensures

positive confirmation to these questions at all stages, a company must identify the critical factors that enable customers to achieve their goals and demonstrate their targeted value, and then it must take action to realize these factors throughout the entire organization.

To achieve this, it is first necessary to collect the customer feedback from different stages and channels into a single center, to convert them into a common language, and to categorize them for use by the whole organization. Steps must be taken to identify the common weaknesses and strengths arising in all channels and to optimize the customer journey and contribute to the total customer experience. Basing the whole organization on this perspective will allow a company to focus on the critical stages that affect customer decisions and to structure and support customer experience in effective and efficient processes.

7.2.2.3. Early Warning System for Uninterrupted Customer Journey

When customer journeys are interrupted and the customer's relation with the brand goes on "stand-by," it is difficult and costly for the company either to replace one customer with another of equal value or to re-establish the relationship with that same customer. Therefore, companies should develop early warning systems to minimize these risks. The presence of early warning systems can ensure that the customer's journey continues uninterrupted, giving the company opportunities to anticipate next steps take necessary measures before hearing unwelcome news from the customer.

Effective early warning systems require that a company identify the critical decision moments in the stages of the customer journey and set company performance standards and metrics within the framework of these critical decision moments. Regular inspections of these performance metrics will identify weaknesses and provide an early warning system indicating that risks of interrupting the customer's journey have increased, which may lead to loss of customers.

7.2.2.4. Targeting of Social Depth at the End of the Customer Journey

The AIDA (Awareness, Interest, Desire, Act) model was developed by Elmo Lewis, one of the most important names in the fields marketing and advertising, back in 1898. In the years since, its definition of the basic steps of the consumer journey has begun to turn into a slightly different structure reflecting conditions today. In the new process, the steps of the consumer's basic journeys are more complex and asymmetric. The 5A model, developed by Kotler, Kartajaya, and Setiawan (2017), conveys this complexity in the simplest form suggested by today's customer dynamics. It transforms the basic steps into Aware—Appeal—Ask—Act—Advocate. Two important differences from the AIDA model are the stages of Ask and Advocate. The Ask step reflects the fact that the consumer's decision is based on the opinions of other consumers. The Advocate step is another way for brands to gain competitive advantage and achieve their strategic goals. When the experiences with the brand lead to high level of commitment, the relationship escalates from being a loyal customer to being a brand advocate. In customer journeys that reach this step, customers share their positive experiences reactively or proactively with other consumers and become advocates for the brand. Consequently, to become a preferred brand in the sea of social reference, which has the greatest influence on the purchasing decisions of consumers today, it is necessary for companies to optimize the architecture and management of customer journeys in parallel with their strategic goals.

8. Conclusion

Today, the most important way for companies to achieve strategic success is to harmonize their organizational structure, business model, and customer approaches with the changing marketing ecosystem, using a holistic perspective. Achieving this strategic objective is possible if the architecture of the neo-consumer's journey with the brand is optimized to create an excellent and unique customer experience.

In the process of this optimization, it is first necessary for the complete organization to adopt a holistic approach, realizing that customers are the most valuable assets of the company, that performance standards should be arranged in harmony with this approach, and that performance metrics should be built around Net Customer Value Added/Loss. Every stage of the customer journey and every contact point should be considered part of the total experience. Focusing these processes on the critical decision points, the company needs to determine the basic success criteria at these points and approach them from the customer's perspective. The final stage of the optimization process is to determine the critical decision moments in the course of the customer journey, create basic performance indicators for these, regularly monitor these indicators, and establish early warning systems to spark intervention in the case of possible weakening.

Brands that successfully optimize the stages of customer journeys create a total customer experience that builds loyal customer groups. These loyal customer groups lead to the rise of consumer-based brand values, which leads to increasing numbers of customers being promoted to brand advocates. Increasing their number of brand advocates and strongly echoing their advocacy in the sea of social reference enables companies to achieve their strategic goals in full compliance with the new ecosystem.

Bibliography

Afra, S. (2014). Dijital Pazarın Odak Noktası e-Ticaret: Dünya'da Türkiye'nin Yeri, Mevcut Durum ve Geleceğe Yönelik Adımlar. İstanbul: TÜSİAD.

Akbay, O. S. (2009). Computerization of Foreign Trade Transactions: A Case Study of Turkey. Trakia Journal of Sciences, 7(3), 43-47.

Altaş, A. (2014). E-Ticaret. İstanbul: Kapital Medya Hizm.

Baaij, M., & Greenven, M. (2004). Persistent Superior Economic Performance, Sustainable Competitive Advantage, and Schumpeterian Innovation:. Leading Established Computer Firms, 1954–2000. European Management Journal, 22(5), 517-531.

Baron, R., & Kenny, D. (1986). The Moderator-Mediator Variable Distinction in Social Psychological Research: Conceptual, Strategic and Statistical Considerations. Journal of Personality and Social Psychology, 6(51), 1173-1182.

Barron, B., Ellsworth, J., & Savetz, K. (1997). Internet Unleashed. (N. Bahar, & D. Türkmen, Çev.) İstanbul: Sistem Yayıncılık.

Bayram, N. (2013). Yapısal Eşitlik Modellemesine Giriş. Bursa: Ezgi Kitapevi.

Bentler, P. M., & Chou, C.-P. (1987). Practical Issues in Structural Modeling. Sociological Methods Research, 16(1), 78-117.

Berry, R. G. (2011). Enhancing Effectiveness on Virtual Teams. Journal of Business Communication, 48(2), 187.

Bliss, J. (2015). Chief Customer Officer 2.0: How To Build Your Customer-Driven Growth Engine. New Jersey: John Wiley and Sons Inc.

Bresnahan, T. F. (2002). Prospects for an Information-Technology-Led Productivity Surge. NBER Innovation Policy & the Economy (MIT Press), 2(1), 135-138.

Brynjolfsson, E. (1993). The productivity paradox of information technology. Communications of the ACM, 36(12), 67-70.

Brynjolfsson, E. (1996). The Contribution of Information Technology to Consumer Welfare. Information Systems Research, 7(3), 281-300.

Brynjolfsson, E., Hitt, L., & Yang, S. (2002). Intangible assets: how computers and organizational structure affect stock market valuations. Brookings Papers on Economic Activity, 1(1), 137-198.

Byrne, B. M. (2010). Structural Equation Modeling with AMOS. New York: Routledge Taylor & Francis Group.

Canpolat, Ö. (2001). E-Ticaret ve Türkiye'deki Gelişmeler. Ankara: Sanayi ve Ticaret Bakanlığı Hukuk Müşavirliği.

Chakraborty, G., Srivastava, P., & Warren, D. (2005). Understanding Corporate B2B Web Sites' Effectiveness from North American and European Perspective. Industrial Marketing Management, 34(5), 420-429.

Chen, J., Chen, Y., Parlar, M., & Xiao, Y. (2011). Optimal inventory and admission policies for drop-shipping retailers serving in-store and online customers. IIE Transactions, 43, 332-347.

Chen, J., Rungruengsamrit, D., Rajkumar, T., & Yen, D. (2013). Success of Electronic Web Sites: A Comparative Study in Two Countries. Information & Management, 50(6), 344-355.

Chuang, S.-H., Liao, C., & Lin, S. (2013). Determinants of knowledge management with information technology support impact on firm performance. Information Technology and Management, 14, 217-230.

Civelek, M. E. (2009). İnternet Çağı Dinamikleri. İstanbul: Beta Basım.

Civelek, M. E., & Sözer, E. G. (2003). İnternet Ticareti: Yeni EkoSosyal Sistem ve Ticaret Noktaları. İstanbul: Beta Basım.

Civelek, M. E., Çemberci, M., Kibritci Artar, O., & Uca, N. (2015). Key Factors of Sustainable Firm Performance: A Strategic Approach. Lincoln: University of Nebraska - Lincoln - Zea Books.

Clemons, E. K., & Row, M. C. (1993). Limits to interfirm coordination through information technology: Results of a field study in consumer goods packaging distribution. Journal of Management Information Systems, 10(1), 73-95.

Çelik, H. E., & Yılmaz, V. (2013). Lisrel 9.1 ile Yapısal Eşitlik Modellemesi. Ankara: Anı Yayıncılık.

Çemberci, M. (2012). Örgütsel Öğrenmenin AR-GE Takımlarının Performansı Üzerine Etkileri. İstanbul: Ati Yayınları.

Çemberci, M. (2012). Tedarik Zinciri Yönetimi Performansının Göstergeleri ve Firma Performansı Üzerine Etkileri: Kavramsal Model Önerisi. İstanbul: Akademi Titiz.

Daft, L. R. (1997). Management. Fort Worth: The Dryden Press.

Daft, L. R. (2004). Organization Theory and Design. Mason: Thomson, South-Western.

Dan, C. (2014). Consumer-To-Consumer (C2C) Electronic Commerce: The Recent Picture. International Journal of Networks and Communications, 4(2), 29-32.

Davesite. (2015). Davesite. 7 21, 2015 The History of the Internet: http://www.davesite.com/webstation/net-history.shtml

Davis, M. F. (2015). Facebook Close Sets Speed Record for $250 Billion Market Cap. 12-01-2015. Bloomberg Technology: http://www.bloomberg.com/news/articles/2015-07-13/facebook-s-close-sets-speed-record-for-250-billion-market-value

DeLone, W. H. (1992). Information systems success: the quest for the dependent variable. Information Systems Research, 3(1), 60-95.

DeLone, W. H., & McLean, E. (2003). The DeLone and McLean Model of Information Systems Success: a Ten-Year Update. Journal of Management Information System, 19(4), 9-30.

Devaraj, S., Fan, M., & Kohli, R. (2002). Antecedents of B2C Channel Satisfaction and Preference: Validating e-Commerce Metrics. Information Systems Research, 13(3), 316-333.

Donaldson, B., Lae, J., & Wright, G. (2012). Strategic and organisational determinants of sophistication in deployed sales force automation systems within three industry sectors in the UK. Journal of Marketing Management, 28(11), 1305-1330.

Dursun, Y., & Kocagöz, E. (2010). Yapısal Eşitlik Modellemesi ve Regresyon: Karşılaştırmalı Bir Analiz. Erciyes Üniversitesi İ.İ.B.F. Dergisi(35), 1-17.

Endsley, M. R., & Kaber, D. (1999). Level of automation effects on performance, situation awareness and workload in a dynamic control task. Ergonomics, 42(3), 462-492.

Flaherty, C., & Lovato, C. (2014). Digital signatures and the Paperless Office. Journal of Internet Law, 17(7), 3-10.

Fornell, C., & Larcker, D. (1981). Evaluating Structural Equation Models with Unobservable Variables and Measurement Error. Journal of Marketing Research, 18(1), 39-50.

Forsythe, S., Liu, C., Shannon, D., & Gardner, L. (2006). Development of a Scale to Measure the Perceived Benefits and Risks of Online Shopping. Journal of Interactive Marketing, 20(2), 55-75.

Gelderman, M. (2002). Task difficulty, task variability and satisfaction with management support systems. Information & Management, 39(7), 593-604.

Genç, N. (2007). Yönetim ve Organizasyon. Ankara: Seçkin Yayıncılık.

Goldman Sachs. (2015). Statista Inc. 03-23-2015. Global retail e-commerce sales volume from 2009 to 2018: www.statista.com/statistics/222128/global-e-commerce-sales-volume-forecast

Grando, A., & Gosso, M. (2005). Electronic Commerce and Logistics: The Last Mile Dilemma Reference Framework and Simulation. Revista de Administração e Inovação, 2(2), 77-97.

Gupta, A. K., & Wilemon, D. (1990). Accelerating the Development of Technology Based New Products. California Management Review, 32(2), 24-44.

Harrison, J., & Wicks, A. (2013). Stakeholder theory, value, and firm performance. Business Ethics Quarterly, 23(1), 97-125.

Hitt, M., Ireland, R., & Hoskisson, R. (1999). Strategic Management: Competitiveness and Globalization. Cincinnati: South-Western College Publishing.

Jayaram, J., Kannan, V., & Tan, K. (2004). Influence of initiators on supply chain value creation. International Journal of Production Research, 42(20), 4377-4399.

Jiang, J., & Klein, G. (2002). Measuring Information Systems Service Quality: Servqual from the Other Side. MIS Quarterly, 26(2), 145-166.

Kang, Y. S., & Kim, Y. (2006). Do visitors Interest Level and Perceived Quantity of Web Page Content Matter in Shaping the Attitude Toward a Web Site? Decision Support Systems, 42(2), 1187-1202.

Kettinger, W., & Lee, C. (1995). Perceived Service Quality and User Satisfaction with the Information Services Function. Decision Sciences, 25(5-6), 737-765.

Khan, M. B., & Matin, M. (2004). Barriers To B2C Segment Of E-Business. Journal of Business & Economics Research, 2(6), 53-60.

Kim, J., Lee, J., Kwanghee, H., & Lee, M. (2002). Business as Buildings: Metrics for the Architectural Quality of Internet Businesses. Information Systems Research, 13(3), 239-254.

Kotler, P., Kartajava, H., & Setiawan, I. (2017). Marketing 4.0: Moving From Traditional to Digital. New Jersey: John Wiley and Sons Inc.

Krause, D. R., Handfield, R., & Scannel , T. (1998). An Empirical Investigation of Supplier Development: Reactive and Strategic Processes. Journal of Operations Management, 17(1), 39-58.

Kulkarni, U. R., Ravindran, S., & Ronald, F. (2007). A Knowledge Management Success Model: Theoretical Development and Empirical Validation. Journal of Management Information Systems, 23(3), 309-347.

Kwon, K. N., & Lee, J. (2003). Concerns About Payment Security of Internet Purchases: A Perspective on Current On-line Shoppers. Clothing Textile Research Journal, 21(4), 174-184.

Laudon, K. C., & Traver, C. (2012). e-Commerce. Harlow: Pearson.

Lee, H. C. (1964). On Information Technology and Organization Structure. Academy of Management Journal, 7(3), 204.

Li, S., & Lin, B. (2006). Accessing Information Sharing and Information Quality in Supply Chain Management. Decision Support Systems, 42, 1641-1656.

Long, M. M., & Chiagouris, L. (2006). The Role of Credibility in Shaping Attitudes Toward Nonprofit Websites. International Journal of Nonprofit and Voluntary Sector Marketing, 11(3), 239-249.

Lu, Y. Y., & Yang, C. (2004). The R&D and Marketing Cooperation Across New Product Development Stages: An Empirical Study of Taiwan's IT Industry. Industrial Marketing Management, 33, 593-605.

McGill, T., & Hobbs, V. (2003). User-Developed Applications and Information Systems Success: A Test of DeLone and McLean's Model. Information Resources Management Journal, 1(16), 24-45.

Meydan, C. H., & Şen, H. (2011). Yapısal Eşitlik Modellemesi AMOS Uygulamaları. Ankara: Detay Yayıncılık.

Mulligan, R. (1999). EDI in foreign trade a perspective on change and international harmonisation. Logistics Information Management, 12(4), 299-309.

OECD. (1999). Economic and Social Impact of Ecommerce: Preliminary Findings and Research Agenda. 03-23-2015. OECD Digital Economy Papers: OECD Publishing: http://dx.doi.org/10.1787/236588526334

Oktal, Ö., & Özata, F. (2013). Bilgi Sistemleri Başarısında Örgütsel Performansı Etkileyen Değişkenlerin İncelenmesi. İ.Ü.İ.F. İşletme İktisadı Enstitüsü Yönetim Dergisi, 24(74), 86-101.

Pagnoni, A., & Visconti, A. (2010). Secure electronic bills of lading: blind counts and digital signatures. Electronic Commerce Research, 10(3), 363-389.

Parasuraman, A., Zeithaml, V., & Malhotra, A. (2005). E-S-QUAL: A Multiple-Item Scale for Assessing Electronic Service Quality. Journal of Service Research, 7(3), 213-233.

Peng, K. F., Fan, Y., & Hsu, T. (2004). Proposing the Content Perception Theory for the Online Content Industry – A Structural Equation Modeling. Industrial Management & Data Systems, 6(104), 469-489.

Perotin, V., & Robinson, A. (2004). Employee Participation, Firm Performance and Survival. Amsterdam: Elsevier JAI.

Petter, S., DeLone , W., & McLean, E. (2008). Measuring Information Systems Success: Models, Dimensions, Measures, and Interrelationships. European Journal of Information Systems, 3(17), 236-263.

Pitt, Pitt, L., Watson, R., & Kavan, C. (1995). Service Quality: A Measure of Information Systems Effectiveness. MIS Quarterly, 19(2), 173-188.

Poirier, C., & Bauer, M. (2001). e-Supply Chain: Using the Internet to Revolutionize your Business. San Francisco: Berrett-Koehler Publishers Inc.

Rai, A., Lang, S., & Welker, R. (2002). Assessing the Validity of IS Success Models: An Empirical Test and Theoretical Analysis. Information System Research, 13(1), 50-69.

Ravichandran, T., Pant, S., & Chatterjee, D. (2007). Impact of industry structure and product characteristics on the structure of B2B vertical hubs. IEEE Transactions on Engineering Management, 54(3), 506-522.

Raykov, T. (1997). Estimation of composite reliability for congeneric measures. Applied Psychological Measurement, 21(2), 173-184.

Sagawa, J. K., & Nagano, M. (2015). Integration, uncertainty, information quality, and performance: a review of empirical research. The International Journal of Advanced Manufacturing Technology, 79(4), 299-308.

Saunders, M., Lewis, P., & Thornhill, A. (2003). Research Methods for Business Students. Essex: Pearson Education Limited.

Schermelleh-Engel, K., Moosbrugger, H., & Müller, H. (2003). Evaluating the Fit of Structural Equation Models: Tests of Significance and Descriptive Goodness-of-Fit Measures. Methods of Psychological Research Online, 8(2), 23-74.

Seddon, P. B. (1997). A Respecification and Extension of the DeLone and McLean Model of IS Success. Information Systems Research, 8(3), 240-253.

Serge. (2015). Web Technologies. Now and tomorrow. 2-18-2016. Atomate: http://atomate.net/blog/web-technologies-now-and-tomorrow/

Sheldon, D. H. (2005). Class A ERP Implementation : Integrating Lean and Six Sigma. Boca Raton: J. Ross Publishing.

Shrivastava, A., & Somasundaram, G. (2009). Information Storage and Management : Storing, Managing, and Protecting Digital Information. Indianapolis: Wiley.

Siau, K., & Tian, Y. (2004). Supply Chains Integration: Architecture and Enabling Technologies. Journal of Computer Information Systems, 44(3), 67-68.

Siebel, T. M. (2001). Taking Care of e-Business. New York: Doubleday.

Sipahi, B., Yurtkoru, E., & Çinko, M. (2010). Sosyal bilimlerde SPSS'le Veri Analizi. İstanbul: Beta Basım A.Ş.

Sonnenberg, S., & Darrow, L. (2011). Straight to the Source: A Guide to Drop-shipping. Springville: Developer Co.

Sözer, E. G. (2009). Postmodern Pazarlama: Marka Çağında Liderlik İçin PIM Modeli. İstanbul: Beta Yayıncılık.

Teo, H. H., Oh, L., & Wei, K. (2003). An Empirical Study of the Effects of Interactivity on Web User Attitude. International Journal of Human-Computer Studies, 58(3), 281-305.

Teo, T. S., & Srivastava, S. (2008). Trust and Electronic Government Success: An Empirical Study. Journal of Management Information Systems, 25(3), 99-132.

Thomas, D., & Griffin, P. (1996). Coordinated Supply Chain Management. European Journal of Operational Research, 94(1), 1-15.

TÜİK. (2014). 2014 Yılı Hanehalkı Bilişim Teknolojileri Kullanım Araştırması. TÜİK.

Wadhwani, R. D. (2012). How Entrepreneurship Forgot Capitalism: Entrepreneurship Teaching and Research in Business Schools. The Fortunes of Capitalism, 49, 223-229.

Wixom, B. H., & Todd, P. (2005). A Theoretical Integration of User Satisfaction and Technology Acceptance. Information Systems Research, 16(1), 85-102.

Wixom, B. H., & Watson, H. (2001). An Empirical Investigation of the Factor Affecting Data Warehousing Success. MIS Quarterly, 1(25), 17-41.

Wu, J.-H. W., & Wang, Y.-M. (2006). Measuring KMS Success: A Respecification of the DeLone and McLean's Model. Information & Management, 43, 728-739.

Yamamoto, G. T. (2013). e-Ticaret. İstanbul: Kriter Yayınları.

Yang, K., Li, X., Kim, H., & Kim, Y. (2015). Social Shopping Website Quality Attributes Increasing Consumer Participation, Positive eWOM, and Co-shopping: The Reciprocating Role of Participation. Journal of Retailing and Consumer Services, 24, 1-9.

Yoo, B., & Donthu, N. (2001). Developing a Scale to Measure Perceived Quality of An Internet Shopping Site. Journal of Electronic Commerce, 2(1), 31-46.

Zhang, P., Dran, G., Blake, P., & Pipithsuksunt, V. (2000). Important Design Features Indifferent Web Site Domains: An Empirical Study of User Perceptions. E-Service Journal, 1(1), 77-91.

www.ingramcontent.com/pod-product-compliance
Lightning Source LLC
Chambersburg PA
CBHW051257050326
40689CB00007B/1226